Ayurveda For Women Wellness

Prof Dr S Mamidanna

SPI PUBLICATIONS

Published by **SPI Publications**, www.spipublications.in
SPI, the **SPI logo**, and **Split Poetry India** are trademarks of **SPI Publications**, or its affiliates.
ISBN-13: 978-93-49860-72-8

First Edition 2025

SPI Publications

Corporate & Editorial Office
117/2, Sector 37, Khandsa Road,
Gurgaon, Haryana 122 001
Phone: +91 98355 52940
Email: contact@spipublications.in
Website: www.spipublications.in

Processed and Printed in India

Copyright

Preface

It's with great happiness that, I would like to acknowledge a great deal of people that get helped me extremely through the entire difficult, challenging, but a rewarding and interesting path towards some sort of Edited Book without having their help and support, none of this work could have been possible.

TABLE OF CONTENTS

Chapter 1: Foundations of Ayurveda

Ayurveda, the ancient science of life that has flourished for over five thousand years, offers a deeply intuitive and holistic understanding of health, harmony, and human nature. Unlike modern systems of medicine that often compartmentalize the body into organs and diseases, Ayurveda views the body as a dynamic, ever-changing interplay of energies governed by universal principles. It is not simply a path to treat illness but a way to live—a philosophy that understands the body as an instrument of nature and the mind as the thread that binds it to the soul. Especially for women, whose bodies are naturally cyclical, nurturing, and responsive to the rhythms of the moon, the insights of Ayurveda offer invaluable guidance for wellness at every stage of life.

The foundation of Ayurveda begins with the understanding that all life is made up of five basic elements—space, air, fire, water, and earth. These elements are not merely symbolic but represent actual principles that can be observed within and outside the human system. In the living body, these five elements combine to form three vital energies known as doshas. Vata, composed of space and air, is the energy of movement. It governs all motion in the body—breathing, blinking, circulation, nerve impulses, and elimination. Pitta, composed of fire and a bit of water, is the energy of transformation. It governs digestion, absorption, metabolism, and the clarity of our thoughts. Kapha, made of earth and water, is the energy of stability and cohesion. It governs lubrication, structure, and growth. Every individual has a unique combination of these three doshas, determined at conception and referred to as their prakriti.

A woman's prakriti is like her energetic fingerprint—completely unique, yet composed of universal patterns. Some women are predominantly Vata, embodying qualities of lightness, creativity, enthusiasm, and sensitivity. Others are primarily Pitta, with sharp intellects, fiery temperaments, and strong determination. Still others are Kapha-dominant, radiating calm, stability, compassion, and patience. Most women are a combination of two doshas, and understanding this constitutional makeup is the first step toward maintaining lifelong health. The Ayurvedic path is never about forcing the body to conform but rather helping it return to its natural balance. By knowing one's prakriti, a woman can make daily choices that support her unique nature—from the food she eats and the herbs she uses to the type of exercise she engages in and the way she rests and rejuvenates.

But health in Ayurveda is not merely defined by the state of the doshas. It is also supported by the integrity of the bodily tissues, the clarity of waste elimination, the strength of digestion, and the purity of the mind. Ayurveda teaches that the body is made of seven dhatus or tissues, which are sequentially nourished from the food we eat. The process begins with rasa, or plasma, which is formed from the digested nutrients and supports the entire body by carrying nourishment. From rasa is formed rakta, or blood, which energizes and oxygenates. Next comes mamsa, or muscle tissue, which provides shape and strength. Meda, or fat tissue, insulates and lubricates. Asthi, or bone, gives structure and support. Majja, or marrow and nerve tissue, governs coordination and sensory function. Finally, shukra in men and artava in women represent the reproductive tissue, which contains the essence of vitality and the capacity for creation.

For women, the artava dhatu plays a particularly central role, not just in fertility but in the overall sense of vitality and emotional well-being. When this tissue is well-nourished, menstruation is healthy, cycles are regular, and hormonal functions are balanced. But when the dhatus are weak, overburdened, or improperly formed due to poor digestion or lifestyle choices, symptoms begin to emerge—irregular periods, painful cramps, hormonal acne, fatigue, or infertility. Ayurveda sees these not merely as conditions to suppress but as signs that the body is no longer able to nourish itself at a deep level. It urges a return to the basics—rekindling digestive fire, choosing foods that suit the doshic balance, eliminating accumulated toxins, and aligning daily routines with nature's rhythms.

The health of the tissues cannot be discussed without acknowledging the waste products of the body—malas—which include urine (mutra), feces (purisha), and sweat (sveda). These are not simply residues to be discarded but are important indicators of internal health. Regular, unobstructed elimination of these malas ensures that the body stays clean, light, and disease-free. When elimination is hindered, due to dehydration, poor eating habits, or emotional stress, toxins build up in the system. This toxic residue, known as ama, is sticky, heavy, and disruptive. It clogs channels, weakens tissues, dulls the mind, and leads to chronic imbalances. The presence of ama can be detected by a coated tongue, foul-smelling stools, bloating, heaviness, and mental fog. Ayurveda places a strong emphasis on digestion and cleansing because it recognizes that even the most nourishing food cannot be transformed into healthy tissue if the digestive fire, or agni, is weak.

Agni is the cornerstone of health in Ayurvedic medicine. Just as a fire transforms raw wood into heat and light, agni transforms food into nutrients, emotions into experiences, and thoughts into understanding. When agni is strong and balanced, the body thrives, the mind is clear, and the immune system is resilient. But when agni is disturbed—too weak, too erratic, or too intense—it sets the stage for disease. Women, whose bodies undergo constant cyclical change, are especially susceptible to fluctuations in agni. During menstruation, pregnancy, postpartum, and menopause, the digestive fire can naturally weaken, requiring conscious attention to food choices, rest, and herbal support.

This ever-changing nature of health is captured in the distinction between prakriti and vikriti. While prakriti is the original constitution with which one is born, vikriti refers to the current state of imbalance. For example, a woman whose original constitution is Kapha may be grounded and nurturing by nature. However, prolonged stress, poor diet, and lack of exercise may push her into a Vata imbalance, leading to anxiety, insomnia, and irregular periods. The goal of Ayurvedic treatment is to bring the individual back to their prakriti, their state of natural balance. Diagnosis in Ayurveda is therefore not just about identifying symptoms but understanding how far a person has drifted from their original nature.

One of the lesser-known but vital components of Ayurvedic anatomy is the concept of srotas, or bodily channels. These channels are responsible for the transportation of nutrients, waste, and energy throughout the body. Just as rivers nourish the land they pass through, srotas nourish the tissues they serve. There are thirteen primary srotas, each associated with a specific function—annavaha for food transport, pranavaha for breath, raktavaha for blood, and so on. For women, the artavavaha srotas, which govern the menstrual and reproductive system, are particularly important. These channels can become blocked due to the accumulation of ama, emotional trauma, hormonal imbalances, or even suppressing natural urges like the need to cry or rest.

When the artavavaha srotas are clear and functional, the menstrual cycle flows smoothly, fertility is enhanced, and the woman experiences a sense of inner radiance. When blocked, the consequences can be wide-ranging—from irregular or painful periods to mood swings, skin eruptions, and even chronic reproductive disorders. Ayurveda offers gentle yet powerful therapies to cleanse and open these channels, including herbal decoctions, steam therapies, oil massages, medicated enemas (basti), and nasal treatments (nasya). These treatments not only clear physical blockages but also help in releasing emotional residues stored in the body.

The path of Ayurvedic healing is not a one-size-fits-all prescription but a deeply personalized journey. It invites each woman to become intimate with her own body, to learn its language, and to honor its signals. Whether it's through observing how her digestion responds to certain foods, how her mood shifts with the seasons, or how her energy rises and falls with the moon, Ayurveda teaches her to see patterns, not problems. Every imbalance is viewed not as a failure, but as a message—a gentle reminder to return home to herself. The Ayurvedic tradition encourages women to see health not as a fixed destination but as a living relationship with the self. This relationship is sustained through daily rituals, seasonal adjustments, and deep listening to the body's subtle signals. When a woman wakes up feeling heavy, dull, or anxious, she is not simply having a "bad day"—she is receiving a message from her inner environment that some aspect of her rhythm has gone out of tune. Ayurveda gives her the vocabulary and tools to decode that message and restore harmony. Whether it is through a warming ginger tea to stoke a sluggish agni, a grounding oil massage to soothe a Vata imbalance, or a quiet walk in nature to cool Pitta agitation, these practices are not just treatments—they are acts of self-love.

The wisdom of Ayurveda lies in its understanding of the cyclical nature of a woman's life. From the onset of menarche through her reproductive years to menopause and beyond, her body is in a state of constant transformation. Each stage brings with it unique challenges and blessings, and Ayurveda offers guidance at every step. In adolescence, the Pitta dosha becomes more active, often leading to acne, irritability, or menstrual irregularity. Rather than suppressing these symptoms, Ayurveda invites a balancing approach—cooling foods, proper rest, gentle routines—to help the young girl transition into womanhood with ease. During the reproductive years, the focus shifts to nurturing artava dhatu, regulating the menstrual cycle, supporting fertility, and ensuring that stress and overwork do not deplete her energy reserves.

Pregnancy, in the Ayurvedic view, is not a medical condition but a sacred and creative process that requires great care, mindfulness, and nourishment. It is a time when the woman is not only creating life within but also undergoing a profound transformation herself. The body, while growing and stretching, becomes more vulnerable, and so the practices of rest, warm foods, self-massage with nourishing oils, and emotional support are all emphasized. Postpartum, the body is considered in a delicate, Vata-sensitive state, and a period of rest and rebuilding is critical. Unfortunately, modern lifestyles often neglect this wisdom, leading to long-term imbalances, fatigue, anxiety, and hormonal dysfunction. Ayurveda reclaims this sacred window of postpartum rejuvenation, offering structured routines to rebuild tissues, restore agni, and re-establish emotional balance.

As a woman approaches menopause, the natural decline in estrogen and progesterone is mirrored by a Vata and Pitta shift in the doshas. Hot flashes, night sweats, insomnia, and emotional turbulence are all seen as manifestations of these shifting energies. Ayurveda doesn't see menopause as a disease to be medicated but as a sacred portal into a new phase of wisdom, clarity, and spiritual growth. With appropriate food, herbs, lifestyle adjustments, and deeper self-reflection, the transition can become a period of empowerment, not suffering. The key, once again, lies in listening to the body's changing needs and making peace with the cyclical nature of life.

The role of the mind is paramount in Ayurvedic wellness. Mental health is not seen as separate from physical health; rather, it is intertwined through every dosha, dhatu, and srotas. Emotions have a direct impact on digestion, immunity, hormonal function, and tissue health. Chronic fear and worry aggravate Vata, leading to dryness, irregularity, and insomnia. Anger and ambition inflame Pitta, triggering hormonal imbalances, acne, or ulcers. Attachment, lethargy, or suppressed grief aggravate Kapha, resulting in stagnation, weight gain, or depression. Ayurveda offers an entire science called Sattvavajaya Chikitsa—healing through the cultivation of clarity, balance, and joy in the mind. This includes not just herbal support for the nervous system but also mantra, meditation, spiritual inquiry, and time in nature.

Women often carry not only their own emotions but also the emotional burdens of family, relationships, and society. These accumulated impressions—samskaras—can lodge in the subtle tissues and create chronic unrest. Ayurveda acknowledges the emotional dimension of health and invites a woman to cleanse her inner world just as regularly as she detoxifies her physical body. Practices like abhyanga (oil massage), nasya (nasal drops), swedana (steam therapy), and shirodhara (oil pouring on the forehead) are not just physical therapies but tools to reset the nervous system and release emotional stagnation. When done with intention, these rituals become a sanctuary where the woman reconnects with her own source of peace.

Another profound gift of Ayurveda is its reverence for the natural world and its rhythms. Ayurveda teaches that the human body is a microcosm of the universe and that our health is intimately tied to the cycles of the moon, sun, and seasons. Just as plants grow, flower, and shed in accordance with the seasons, so do we. For women, this relationship is even more direct, as their menstrual cycles often reflect lunar patterns. When a woman lives out of sync with these rhythms—staying up late, eating unseasonal food, ignoring the need for rest during her period—imbalance is inevitable. Dinacharya (daily routines) and ritucharya (seasonal routines) are not restrictive systems but gentle frameworks that help the body remain in harmony with nature.

Waking before sunrise, cleansing the body, practicing self-massage, eating at regular intervals, honoring the natural transitions between seasons—these simple rituals have a powerful cumulative effect. They stabilize the doshas, protect agni, and create a container of order and rhythm in which healing can unfold. Ayurveda recognizes that healing is not achieved through quick fixes or isolated interventions but through a consistent, nurturing relationship with the self. This relationship is forged day by day, breath by breath, moment by moment.

Food, in the Ayurvedic view, is not just fuel but medicine. It carries the intelligence of nature and has the power to either nourish or deplete, depending on how, when, and what we eat. A woman's diet must be in alignment with her doshic balance, season, age, activity level, and emotional state.

Heavy, oily foods may ground a Vata woman in winter but overwhelm her digestion in summer. Spicy, sour, and fermented foods may ignite passion and ambition in a Pitta woman but also trigger skin eruptions or irritability. Sweet, dense, and cold foods may comfort a Kapha woman but also dull her mind and slow her metabolism. Awareness of these nuances allows her to make food choices that support balance rather than create conflict.

Moreover, the way food is prepared and consumed matters. Ayurveda places great emphasis on mindful cooking and eating. Food should be cooked fresh, with love and attention, and eaten in a calm atmosphere. Eating while standing, scrolling through the phone, or watching distressing news disrupts digestion and creates emotional ama. Chewing thoroughly, savoring flavors, expressing gratitude—all these simple practices turn meals into healing rituals. Certain spices like ginger, cumin, fennel, turmeric, and cardamom are used not just for taste but for their medicinal qualities. When used wisely, these spices kindle digestion, reduce bloating, detoxify the liver, and enhance clarity of mind.

Ayurveda also emphasizes fasting and detox at appropriate intervals to cleanse the body of accumulated ama. This does not mean extreme restriction but gentle purification through warm water, simple foods, digestive teas, and rest. For women, these practices must be timed carefully—not during menstruation, pregnancy, or times of emotional vulnerability. The female body is already doing the work of monthly cleansing through menstruation, and additional purgation must be done under guidance and only when the system is stable.

This level of nuanced care is what sets Ayurveda apart. It sees health as dynamic, responsive, and relational. It respects the complexity of women's bodies and honors the sacredness of their life transitions. A woman is not a problem to be fixed or a case to be managed—she is a living system of intelligence that, when aligned with nature, becomes a source of vitality, creativity, and joy.

Chapter 2: Ayurvedic View on Women's Physiology

Ayurveda offers a timeless, compassionate, and profoundly intuitive understanding of the female body—an understanding that is not limited to anatomy or hormones, but one that perceives the woman as a complete embodiment of nature itself. Rooted in the rhythms of the moon, earth, and cosmos, the female body is seen as both deeply sacred and subtly complex. While modern medicine focuses primarily on the mechanical and hormonal aspects of the female physiology, Ayurveda goes deeper into the energetic, elemental, emotional, and cyclical dimensions of womanhood. It sees women not as a set of organs or symptoms but as a living system of intelligence designed to nurture, adapt, and evolve. Her body is a dynamic microcosm of nature, and her health is best maintained not through force or control but through understanding, rhythm, and harmony.

From the earliest Ayurvedic texts such as the Charaka Samhita and Sushruta Samhita, it is clear that the ancient sages had a deep appreciation for the uniqueness of the female physiology. They emphasized the special role of *artava dhatu*—the reproductive tissue unique to women—and explored how menstruation, pregnancy, and menopause are not merely biological occurrences but transitions marked by profound energetic shifts. Female physiology is defined by softness, fluidity, and receptivity, governed primarily by the water and earth elements. These elements give women their capacity to create, to nourish, and to sustain life. They also bring greater emotional depth, sensitivity to environment, and a heightened intuitive awareness.

At the heart of Ayurveda's view of physiology is the concept of *doshas*—Vata, Pitta, and Kapha—which represent the elemental energies governing all biological processes. Every woman has her own unique ratio of these doshas, known as her *prakriti*, which determines her natural constitution. Some women are Vata-dominant, thin, light, and expressive, with quick minds and creative energy. Others are Pitta-dominant, with sharp intellects, strong digestion, and leadership qualities. Kapha-dominant women tend to be nurturing, calm, emotionally stable, and physically well-built. While prakriti remains constant throughout life, temporary imbalances—or *vikriti*—can cause disharmony, especially in the reproductive and emotional systems.

The female body, unlike the male, is cyclic in nature. It is not designed to function in a straight line of constant performance. Instead, it flows through phases that repeat themselves: the menstrual cycle, the lunar rhythm, the hormonal fluctuations of pregnancy, the stillness of menopause. This cyclical pattern reflects the very essence of creation and dissolution. Ayurveda sees these cycles not as inconveniences to be managed, but as opportunities for renewal and alignment. The menstrual cycle, for instance, is not just a biological process of shedding the uterine lining—it is a monthly purification that supports emotional release, detoxification, and energetic reset. It allows the body to cleanse itself physically and emotionally, preparing for the next wave of creation.

Each phase of the menstrual cycle corresponds with the dominance of a particular dosha. In the first half of the cycle, after menstruation, Kapha energy builds. This phase is slow, heavy, and nourishing, supporting the rebuilding of tissues and preparing the body for ovulation. A woman often feels more emotionally grounded, physically stable, and socially connected during this time. Ovulation, marked by a sharp release of the egg and peak fertility, is governed by Pitta dosha. The body becomes warmer, more energetic, and focused. Libido increases, and the mind is often sharper. But if Pitta is excessive, it can bring irritability, acne, and inflammation. After ovulation, the body moves into the Vata phase, as space and air elements increase. This is the time of emotional introspection, increased sensitivity, and preparation for menstruation. If Vata becomes aggravated, it may result in bloating, anxiety, irregular periods, or painful cramps.

When the cycle begins, the body shifts into detox mode. Menstruation is Vata-predominant, and Ayurveda recommends rest, warmth, and light nourishment during these days. Excessive activity, cold foods, or emotional stimulation can disturb the process, leading to longer-term imbalances. The ancient wisdom advises that women take this time to slow down, reflect, and conserve energy. While modern life may not always allow for seclusion or stillness during menstruation, even small adjustments—like reducing workload, minimizing cold exposure, or practicing self-care—can support this natural process.

The balance of hormones in a woman's body is not a standalone biochemical issue in Ayurveda—it is a direct expression of doshic harmony, digestive fire (*agni*), and emotional state. When agni is strong, food is digested well, tissues are nourished, and ojas—the vital essence responsible for immunity, fertility, and glow—is preserved. Weak digestion or chronic ama (toxins) buildup can obstruct the flow of hormones and disturb the endocrine system. Hence, many hormonal conditions such as PCOS, thyroid dysfunction, painful periods, or early menopause are treated in Ayurveda not through hormone replacement but by rekindling agni, purifying ama, balancing doshas, and strengthening dhatus (tissues).

Moreover, Ayurveda strongly emphasizes the link between emotional health and reproductive physiology. The heart (*hridaya*) and the uterus (*yoni*) are said to be connected through a subtle channel called *manovaha srotas*. When the mind is burdened with stress, unresolved emotions, or excessive stimulation, the flow of prana (life force) between these centers is disrupted. This manifests physically in the form of irregular menses, reproductive fatigue, or fertility challenges. This is why mental clarity, emotional expression, and inner peace are not luxuries in Ayurvedic care for women—they are necessities.

Traditional Ayurvedic care for emotional balance includes sattvic diet (pure, fresh, seasonal food), medhya herbs (Brahmi, Shankhpushpi, Jatamansi), aromatic therapies, and practices like yoga, pranayama, and meditation. A woman is encouraged to cultivate *sattva*, the mental quality of peace, clarity, and compassion. Sattva is the antidote to *rajas* (overactivity, passion, restlessness) and *tamas* (inertia, confusion, depression), which are often at the root of emotional disorders. Practices that bring sattva include gentle movement, devotional practices, time in nature, journaling, gratitude, and balanced relationships. Ayurvedic emotional healing is never about suppression—it is about understanding, honoring, and transmuting emotions into wisdom.

This understanding brings us to the heart of Ayurveda's perspective on womanhood: *Stree Swabhava*. The natural qualities of a woman are seen not as weaknesses to be overcome, but as innate strengths to be celebrated. According to classical Ayurvedic philosophy, women are more aligned with lunar energy—the energy of change, intuition, coolness, and receptivity. This lunar nature makes them deeply empathic, intuitive, nurturing, and capable of withstanding emotional and physical adversity with grace. They are reservoirs of *ojas*, and their energy has a healing effect on families and societies.

Stree swabhava includes qualities like adaptability, softness, devotion, creativity, inner strength, and emotional intelligence. A woman who lives in harmony with her swabhava does not need to compete, control, or suppress her nature to succeed. She thrives when she can express her full self in an environment that respects rhythm, nurtures rest, and values authenticity. The modern world often demands that women remain in a constant Pitta state—performing, achieving, and outpacing their limits. But Ayurveda calls for a return to their true selves. It says: you are not here to prove your worth—you are here to embody your truth.

When a woman lives against her nature—eating fast food in a rush, ignoring her cycles, staying up late under artificial lights, suppressing her emotions, or over-identifying with roles and expectations—her system begins to fragment. Fatigue sets in. Sleep is disturbed. Skin loses its glow. Fertility declines. Mood swings increase. Digestion weakens. This is not a failure of the body but a signal. A message from within saying, "Come back." Ayurveda offers that return—a path back to self-connection, self-trust, and self-nourishment.

Whether she is bleeding, ovulating, pregnant, birthing, nursing, or transitioning through menopause, Ayurveda reminds the woman that she is a reflection of nature's intelligence. She is not linear; she is spiral. Not static; but cyclical. She is capable of fierce strength and profound softness, and her well-being depends on how well she honors both. No matter what stage she is in, no matter how long she has been out of balance, healing is always possible—because she carries within her the same force that governs the cosmos: the force of rhythm, the power of balance, the intelligence of life.

Chapter 3: Lifecycle Care in Ayurveda,

Ayurveda views the journey of a woman's life as a graceful unfolding, not marked simply by age but by phases of transformation—each imbued with its own needs, energies, and spiritual significance. At the core of this vision lies the understanding that the female body is not static but constantly adapting, cycling through phases of birth, development, reproduction, decline, and renewal. Unlike linear models that define aging as deterioration, Ayurveda honors life as a spiral, where each turn offers new potential for deeper awareness, refined vitality, and inner growth. For women especially, this cyclical nature is apparent not just in their reproductive capabilities, but in the way they relate to time, emotions, and energy. From the awakening of adolescence to the fullness of reproduction, the sacred vessel of pregnancy and birth, and the reflective season of menopause, Ayurveda provides a path for the conscious care of a woman's body, mind, and soul at every stage.

In adolescence, known in Ayurveda as *Kumarika Avastha*, the subtle transition from girlhood to womanhood begins. This is a time of great sensitivity and expansion, as the doshas begin to express themselves more dynamically, hormonal pathways activate, and reproductive tissues like *Artava Dhatu* start to mature. The adolescent girl experiences an influx of Vata and Pitta, creating a landscape that is both delicate and fiery. Vata governs growth, nervous system sensitivity, and the emergence of creativity and imagination. Pitta initiates the fire of transformation—bringing clarity, ambition, intellect, but also irritability and inflammation when out of balance. These years often come with irregular menstrual cycles, skin eruptions, digestive fluctuations, and emotional instability. Ayurveda does not pathologize these changes but considers them a natural part of internal evolution. The goal is not to suppress them, but to support the girl in learning how to align with her own body's wisdom.

This is a time when the mother, elder sister, or a wise mentor plays a crucial role. She is meant to gently guide the girl into understanding her inner world. Teaching her how to eat according to her dosha, how to rest, how to cleanse, and how to embrace her menstrual cycle with reverence is one of the most important initiations a girl can receive. If she is encouraged to fear or resent her bleeding, she may develop a negative relationship with her body. If, instead, she is taught to see menstruation as sacred, rhythmic, and powerful, she steps into her womanhood with pride, dignity, and clarity. Ayurveda recommends a sattvic lifestyle during adolescence—fresh, warm foods, a focus on greens, fruits, ghee, and lentils, moderate exercise, limited screen time, and deep sleep. Herbs like Brahmi and Guduchi support the nervous system and immunity, while Shatavari and Lodhra gently nourish reproductive tissues.

As the adolescent matures, she enters *Ritumati Avastha*, or the fertile, reproductive phase of life. This is a period marked by energy, ambition, emotional depth, and often, increased responsibilities. Whether the woman is focused on career, marriage, family, or self-discovery, her body is in a state of peak productivity. Ovulation and menstruation occur rhythmically, the hormones fluctuate monthly, and the reproductive tissues are in full function. The balance of the three doshas becomes more dynamic during this phase. Vata governs the movement of eggs, menstruation, and the flow of emotions. Pitta manages digestion, metabolism, hormonal conversion, and passion. Kapha ensures lubrication, tissue nourishment, and fertility. If this balance is disrupted, disorders like PMS, painful periods, polycystic ovarian syndrome (PCOS), endometriosis, fibroids, or emotional mood swings may develop.

During the reproductive years, many women stretch themselves thin—between work, family, social demands, and personal aspirations. In doing so, they may ignore the small whispers of their body: the slight fatigue before menstruation, the digestive heaviness after a hurried meal, the emotional lowness during ovulation. Over time, these whispers become symptoms, and the symptoms evolve into chronic conditions. Ayurveda teaches that these signs are not interruptions but signals—guides to return to self-awareness. The menstrual cycle is viewed as a monthly report card of a woman's health. When cycles are irregular, heavy, painful, or absent, it is not just a reproductive issue but a sign that some deeper imbalance—either digestive, emotional, or energetic—is at play.

Fertility in Ayurveda is not reduced to the capacity to conceive but is understood as a state of internal richness, ojas, and creative energy. A fertile woman radiates vitality. Her skin glows, her digestion is strong, her mind is calm, and her emotions are clear. She need not wish for a child to express her fertility—it is the creative force that allows her to birth ideas, projects, relationships, and dreams. When conception is desired, Ayurveda offers time-tested methods to cleanse and prepare the body, including Panchakarma for detoxification, ojas-enhancing foods like milk, ghee, saffron, and almonds, and herbs like Ashwagandha, Shatavari, and Vidari. The focus is to build strong reproductive tissues, eliminate toxins, calm the mind, and align the couple with each other emotionally and spiritually.

Then comes the deeply sacred stage of *Garbha*—pregnancy—and *Sutika Paricharya*—the postnatal phase. In Ayurveda, pregnancy is seen as a time when the soul and matter come together. The woman becomes the bridge between worlds. Her body is not only growing a child but also becoming a new version of herself. The doshic energies shift toward Kapha, as the body builds tissues, stores nutrients, and nourishes both the fetus and the mother. Pregnancy is not a condition to be feared but a sacred state to be respected. A pregnant woman is advised to eat simply and richly—cooked rice, mung dal, milk, ghee, root vegetables, and gentle herbal preparations to support digestion, immunity, and emotional stability. Her thoughts and emotions are considered as impactful as her food. Hence, she is guided to read uplifting stories, avoid disturbing news, and surround herself with kindness, music, and beauty.

The connection between mother and fetus is energetic. Ayurveda emphasizes that the child receives impressions through the mother's state of mind. This practice of *Garbha Sanskar* means the education and emotional shaping of the fetus begins in the womb. A peaceful mother births a peaceful child. A loved mother births a child rooted in love. This is not philosophy but lived experience. From the sixth month onward, the fetus is said to develop more awareness of sound, light, and touch, and hence the mother is asked to treat herself with the same tenderness she would give her child.

After delivery, the mother enters a Vata-dominated phase. There is space where there was once form, dryness where there was once nourishment, and sensitivity where there was once stability. Ayurveda views the *Sutika Kala* as a vital phase that determines the woman's long-term physical and emotional health. If care is not given in this phase, complications like postpartum depression, back pain, hormonal imbalances, chronic fatigue, or anxiety may linger for years. Traditionally, the mother is supported by family or a doula, given warm oil massages, bathed with herbal decoctions, fed soups, broths, and nourishing teas, and encouraged to rest deeply. Herbal medicines like Dashamoolarishta, Jeerakarishtam, and Rasayanas are administered to rejuvenate tissues and support lactation. Gentle yoga, meditation, prayer, and chanting help her reclaim her space in the world—not as a broken body needing repair, but as a powerful soul who has undergone a sacred transformation.

The world rarely sees motherhood this way today. The pressure to "bounce back," to work, to host guests, or to take care of others denies the mother the full sanctity of her healing. Ayurveda offers her a different reality—one where her needs are sacred, where her softness is not weakness, and where her nourishment is a priority for the health of the next generation.

As time flows, the body begins to change again. Menstruation slows, the ovaries quieten, and the hormones shift. This is the beginning of *Vriddhavastha*—the phase of menopause and aging. In the West, menopause is often seen as a biological shutdown, a hormonal crisis, or an emotional decline. Ayurveda, however, views it as a transition into wisdom. The body is moving away from reproduction toward introspection. The cycles stop, not because life is ending, but because a new form of life—one oriented inward—is beginning. This stage is again dominated by Vata—marked by dryness, irregularity, and subtlety. Symptoms such as hot flashes, joint pain, forgetfulness, insomnia, anxiety, and fatigue are common if Vata is not grounded and Pitta is not cooled.

But menopause is not a problem to solve—it is a passage to honor. The woman is now the wise elder, the grandmother, the keeper of memory and tradition. Her value lies not in productivity, but in presence. Her body may be less active, but her spirit is more awake. Ayurveda supports this time through warmth—internal and external. Warm, nourishing foods, oil massages, gentle movement, spiritual practice, and community support are essential. Herbs like Shatavari, Licorice, Bala, and Guggulu help to balance Vata and Pitta, reduce inflammation, and support bone and joint health.

Emotionally, menopause is often a time of grief, reflection, and realignment. The roles the woman once carried—of mother, wife, professional—may be shifting or dissolving. She is faced with new questions: Who am I now? What is my purpose? What have I learned? This is not a crisis but a turning inward, a necessary pause to listen to the inner voice that was perhaps ignored during the busyness of life. Ayurveda encourages her to embrace this stillness, to spend time in solitude, in prayer, in creativity, or in service. Her health now depends more on her state of mind than her hormones. The more she lives in alignment with her truth, the more radiant her later years become.

Throughout all these stages—adolescence, reproductive maturity, pregnancy and motherhood, menopause and elderhood—Ayurveda offers not just treatment but guidance. It provides a gentle hand on the shoulder of every woman, reminding her that she is not broken, not incomplete, and not alone. She is a cycle of nature itself, and when she lives in harmony with this cycle, her life becomes a dance of health, joy, and wisdom.

Chapter 4: Common Women's Disorders and Ayurvedic Solutions,

In a world increasingly driven by speed, external validation, and disconnection from natural rhythms, the female body often becomes a quiet casualty. The ancient science of Ayurveda, however, provides a compassionate lens through which the suffering that women experience—whether physical, emotional, or energetic—is not merely to be corrected but deeply understood. Disorders in Ayurveda are not abrupt intrusions; they are messages. They are invitations to pause, to feel, to inquire. When a woman experiences irregular menstruation, hormonal chaos, fertility issues, emotional overwhelm, or menopausal disorientation, Ayurveda teaches her not to reject the body but to turn inward and listen—to her lifestyle, her digestion, her thoughts, her pace of living. Through this deeper listening, healing becomes possible—not as a surface adjustment but as a return to wholeness.

Menstrual health, in this context, is not just a monthly event but a mirror of a woman's inner state. Ayurveda regards the menstrual cycle as a natural cleansing process—a built-in detox that occurs every month, reflecting the state of doshas, agni (digestive fire), emotional health, and reproductive strength. When this rhythm is disturbed, Ayurveda sees it not merely as a gynecological issue but as a sign of misalignment in multiple systems. Polycystic Ovarian Syndrome (PCOS), for instance, which now affects a growing number of young women, is more than just cysts on ovaries or irregular ovulation. It is a reflection of disturbed Kapha in the form of accumulation and congestion, often combined with Vata's irregularity and Pitta's metabolic intensity. The modern sedentary lifestyle, constant stress, late meals, refined sugars, and mental fatigue only exacerbate the condition.

Ayurvedic management of PCOS begins with correcting metabolism. Digestive fire must be kindled, ama must be cleared, and hormonal pathways need to be purified. Herbs such as Triphala, Trikatu, Guggulu, and Guduchi are often used for detoxification. A Kapha-reducing diet—warm, dry, spiced foods in moderation with minimal dairy, wheat, and sugar—is prescribed. Daily exercise is not just recommended—it is vital. Vata must also be calmed with routine, warm oil massages, and adequate sleep. Emotional healing is central. Many women with PCOS carry a history of overexertion, perfectionism, or emotional suppression. Once the systems slow down, breathe, and find a new rhythm, the body responds. Cycles become more predictable. Ovulation returns. Energy stabilizes. Weight shifts gently. But it is not a quick fix. It is a re-education in living in harmony with one's self.

Dysmenorrhea, or painful menstruation, is another condition Ayurveda treats with deep reverence and understanding. Pain is the body's way of calling attention to blocked energy. In Ayurveda, this blockage is often due to aggravated Vata in the pelvic region. Vata brings coldness, dryness, constriction, and irregularity. In the context of menstruation, this leads to cramping, bloating, nervousness, lower back pain, and fatigue. The pain is often worsened by cold exposure, erratic schedules, caffeine, or emotional tension. Ayurveda recommends reducing Vata through warmth, oiliness, and stillness. A few days before menstruation, the woman is encouraged to shift her routine—to eat lighter, warmer foods, avoid raw vegetables or ice-cold drinks, reduce stimulation, and engage in nourishing rituals like abhyanga (self-massage with sesame oil), gentle stretching, or journaling. Herbs such as Dashamoola, Hingvastak, and Shatavari can soothe the uterus and reduce spasms. But above all, Ayurveda invites the woman to rest during her period—not just physically, but emotionally. This is not a time to push, perform, or engage in intense activity. It is a time to receive, to release, and to return to herself.

On the opposite end of the spectrum lies amenorrhea—the absence of menstruation. This condition, while sometimes physiological during pregnancy or breastfeeding, is a concern when it arises from imbalance. Amenorrhea may result from excessive Vata (due to overthinking, under-eating, over-exercising), disturbed Pitta (due to inflammation or autoimmune conditions), or Kapha blockage (often tied to obesity or sluggish metabolism). Ayurveda addresses amenorrhea by first identifying the type of doshic disturbance and then restoring harmony. If Vata is at play, the woman is guided to rest, rebuild her ojas, and nourish herself deeply—emotionally and physically. Foods are rich, warm, and oily, with sweet, grounding tastes. Emotional safety and reducing performance pressure are equally important. If Kapha is dominant, the body must be lightened—cleansing therapies like Vamana (emetic therapy) or Basti (enemas) are used cautiously under supervision. Herbs like Kumari (aloe vera), Shatavari, and Lodhra stimulate menstrual flow and nourish reproductive tissues. Once the internal space is restored—when nourishment flows, and the nervous system feels safe—the cycle often returns gently, like a river finding its way back to its course.

Perhaps no condition reflects the convergence of body, mind, and spirit more than infertility. For a woman longing for conception, infertility can be deeply wounding—not just physically but psychologically. Ayurveda's understanding of infertility is holistic and compassionate. It acknowledges that fertility is not simply a biological function but an expression of health on all levels. A fertile woman is not just able to conceive—she is energetically abundant. Her reproductive tissues are well-nourished, her ojas is full, her emotions flow without suppression, and her mind is peaceful. Fertility is not created; it is revealed when obstructions—physical or emotional—are removed.

Ayurveda first cleanses the channels of the body through therapies like Virechana and Basti. Then, *Rasayana* therapy is administered to rejuvenate tissues. Foods that build ojas—milk, dates, ghee, almonds, saffron, root vegetables—are emphasized. Herbs like Shatavari, Ashwagandha, Gokshura, and Bala support ovulation, uterine tone, and hormonal balance. But the most subtle and powerful aspect of treatment lies in the woman's relationship with herself. Often, infertility is not a defect to be repaired but a call to deeper alignment. Is she constantly pushing herself? Is her life rhythm aligned with nature? Is she nourished emotionally? Is there unresolved grief or fear? Ayurveda opens space for these inquiries, holding the woman not as a "case" but as a sacred being in transition. When healing begins from this place, fertility often becomes a natural, effortless extension of health.

Menopause, another profound transition, brings its own terrain of change. It marks the end of menstruation, but not the end of vitality. In Ayurveda, menopause is known as a Vata-predominant phase, with possible Pitta or Kapha involvement depending on the symptoms. The drying nature of Vata can bring insomnia, joint pain, thinning of tissues, and emotional fragility. Pitta's heat may cause hot flashes, irritability, and anger. Kapha may manifest as depression, weight gain, or brain fog. The treatment is not hormone replacement but the gentle invitation to recalibrate. Women are encouraged to shift their diet to moist, warm, easy-to-digest meals. Nightshade vegetables, alcohol, and spicy foods are minimized. Herbs such as Shatavari, Brahmi, Licorice, and Jatamansi are included to soothe the nervous system, support estrogen-like activity, and balance sleep and mood.

Equally important is the internal perspective. Menopause is not a collapse—it is a calling. It is a time to turn inward, to deepen spiritual life, to reflect on the wisdom gained, and to shed old identities. Women are guided to embrace meditation, prayer, creative pursuits, and time in nature. The body is not betraying her—it is simply changing form. And with support, this change becomes a flowering of insight, serenity, and grace.

Behind all these physical transformations lies the vast domain of mental and emotional health. Ayurveda recognizes that the *Manovaha Srotas*—the channel of the mind—is just as real and susceptible to imbalance as any organ or tissue. Women, due to their natural sensitivity and emotional intelligence, are particularly affected by disharmony in this domain. Whether it is anxiety, depression, mood swings, or emotional burnout, Ayurveda does not see these as weaknesses but as imbalances needing to be soothed, not suppressed.

Chronic stress, irregular routines, excessive stimulation, or emotional repression aggravate Vata in the mind—leading to racing thoughts, restlessness, and insomnia. Excess Pitta brings perfectionism, criticism, anger, and burnout. Kapha leads to emotional heaviness, attachment, and inertia. The first step in Ayurvedic emotional healing is *Ahara*—not just food for the body, but food for the mind. This includes what one reads, watches, thinks, and absorbs. Sattvic inputs—like positive company, music, spiritual teachings, and nature—begin to purify the mind. Regular meals, adequate sleep, and simple living anchor the nervous system. Herbs like Brahmi, Ashwagandha, Tagara, and Mandukaparni rejuvenate the mind and restore balance.

But true healing often happens through ritual. Ayurveda invites the woman to return to herself through rhythm. A warm oil massage before a bath. A cup of spiced milk before bed. A short breathing practice at sunrise. Silence for a few minutes each day. These are not acts of indulgence; they are medicine. They tell the nervous system: you are safe. They tell the mind: you are enough. They tell the soul: you are seen.

When a woman chooses to heal in this way—not through force, but through rhythm—not through rejection, but through compassion—something profound begins to shift.

Her symptoms no longer control her. Her body is no longer a battlefield. Her cycles, her emotions, her transitions—they all become guides. And Ayurveda, in its gentle, rooted wisdom, becomes her companion—not promising instant fixes but offering something more powerful: the path back to her center.

Chapter 5: Ayurvedic Herbs and Rasayana for Women,

In the vast and living system of Ayurveda, the role of herbs is not to act merely as pharmacological agents, but as conscious elements of nature, carefully attuned to the rhythms of the body and mind. Each herb in Ayurveda is believed to possess not just a chemical profile, but also a personality, an energy, and a subtle effect that reaches deeper than the physical body. For women, whose health is governed by cycles—of hormones, of emotions, of life transitions—these herbs offer the possibility of not just relief, but restoration. Restoration of rhythm. Restoration of trust in the body. Restoration of energy that flows without fear or fatigue. The Ayurvedic tradition of *Rasayana* holds the key to this restoration. It is not a quick-fix remedy; it is a philosophy of longevity, resilience, nourishment, and the fullness of life. It teaches that rejuvenation is not indulgence—it is intelligence. That for a woman to live well, she must be nourished from the inside out.

At the heart of Rasayana lie the herbs that help build *ojas*—the essence of vitality, immunity, and radiance. Ojas is what makes a woman glow from within. It is the invisible thread that connects physical strength, emotional stability, and spiritual depth. It is what allows her to handle life's changes without falling apart. Among the most revered herbs for building ojas is Shatavari. This graceful, cooling, and nurturing root supports women through every stage of life—puberty, menstruation, fertility, pregnancy, postpartum, and menopause. It is sweet in taste, heavy in quality, and cooling in potency, making it ideal for pacifying aggravated Pitta and Vata. Shatavari helps build healthy *Artava dhatu* (reproductive tissue), supports the uterus, balances estrogen, and calms emotional turbulence. It is not a stimulant—it works slowly and deeply, reminding the body how to hold itself with strength and softness at the same time.

Taken with milk or ghee, Shatavari becomes a Rasayana par excellence. It supports not just hormonal function, but emotional grace. Women who feel depleted, anxious, overworked, or disconnected from their inner voice often benefit greatly from this herb. It allows the nervous system to unwind and the reproductive system to remember its rhythm. As a galactagogue, it also supports lactation, making it invaluable in postpartum care. In menopause, it soothes hot flashes, dryness, and restlessness. Its influence is not limited to the uterus—it nourishes all tissues through its ojas-building effect.

Complementing Shatavari in the Rasayana tradition is Ashwagandha, another revered herb that strengthens the body and calms the mind. While often marketed as a male herb, Ashwagandha has immense benefits for women—especially those who suffer from anxiety, exhaustion, adrenal fatigue, or poor sleep. It is warming and strengthening, improving resistance to stress and rebuilding depleted *majja dhatu* (nerve tissue). For women constantly "on," juggling work, family, social roles, and personal ambitions, Ashwagandha offers grounding. It slows the overactive mind, nourishes the adrenal glands, and restores deep sleep. When taken with warm milk and honey at night, it becomes a balm for the entire system—repairing what has been frayed, burned out, or over-extended.

Ayurveda also places great importance on Bala, a herb whose very name means "strength." Bala enhances muscle tone, supports joint flexibility, and rejuvenates the nervous system. It is ideal for women recovering from childbirth, surgery, or long illness. Used in medicated oils, Bala is massaged into the skin to restore nerve function, relieve pain, and replenish lost strength. Internally, it builds stamina and supports uterine tone. In a society that rarely allows time for full recovery, Bala offers the promise of complete rejuvenation—not just functioning again, but thriving again.

Other important Rasayana herbs for women include Guduchi (Tinospora cordifolia), Amalaki (Indian Gooseberry), and Haritaki. Guduchi is especially renowned for its immune-modulating properties. It is bitter, light, and cooling—perfect for clearing low-grade inflammation, chronic fatigue, skin issues, and autoimmune tendencies. Amalaki is the richest natural source of vitamin C, and in Ayurveda, it is one of the only fruits that balances all three doshas. It supports digestion, liver health, blood purification, and hormonal balance. Combined with other herbs in the famous Rasayana formulation *Chyawanprash*, Amalaki becomes a daily elixir for energy, clarity, and immunity. Haritaki, though more known for its laxative and cleansing properties, is also a subtle rejuvenator—especially for the colon and mind. It supports elimination, clears stagnation, and increases absorption of nutrients.

In a world that constantly demands output, performance, and multitasking from women, the body's response is often chronic stress. Ayurveda acknowledges this through the inclusion of adaptogens—herbs that help the body adapt to stress, restore equilibrium, and increase resilience without overstimulation. Brahmi (Bacopa monnieri) is perhaps the most well-known adaptogen for the mind. It is a medhya Rasayana—one that nourishes the mind, enhances memory, and calms the emotions. It is sattvic in nature, meaning it promotes peace, clarity, and spiritual awareness. For women who feel overwhelmed, forgetful, restless, or anxious, Brahmi offers calm without sedation. When taken regularly with ghee, it sharpens mental faculties while softening emotional intensity.

Shankhpushpi, often paired with Brahmi, is another deeply cooling herb that soothes the nervous system. It is ideal for women who experience insomnia, hormonal anxiety, or PMS-related mood swings. Jatamansi, also known as the "herb of inner silence," is a fragrant root that calms the mind and strengthens the heart. It is especially useful for women who are grieving, emotionally fragile, or highly sensitive to emotional fluctuations. Together, these herbs offer not just stress relief, but a realignment of the mind with the deeper self.

Tulsi, or Holy Basil, is an adaptogen rooted in both the medicinal and spiritual traditions of India. Beyond its role in clearing respiratory congestion, Tulsi is a heart-opener and mood elevator. It helps regulate cortisol, reduce sugar cravings, and lift the emotional fog that often clouds modern life. A daily cup of Tulsi tea can act as both a ritual and a remedy—a reminder to pause, breathe, and return to center. Licorice (Yashtimadhu), with its sweet taste and cooling energy, balances Vata and Pitta. It supports adrenal recovery, soothes mucous membranes, and enhances complexion. Though it should be used cautiously in cases of high blood pressure, Licorice is an excellent support for hormonal clarity and emotional sweetness.

When addressing reproductive health, Ayurveda draws upon a treasury of herbs that support the *Artavavaha srotas*—the subtle channels of the reproductive system. Alongside Shatavari, herbs like Ashoka, Lodhra, and Kumari (Aloe Vera) are foundational. Ashoka bark, often formulated in *Ashokarishta*, is a powerful Pitta-balancer for the uterus. It regulates menstrual flow, reduces pain, and strengthens uterine walls. Lodhra is astringent and cooling, ideal for excessive bleeding, leucorrhea, or inflammatory gynecological conditions. Kumari is a rejuvenator for the liver and reproductive system alike. Taken fresh as juice or in formulations like *Kumaryasava*, it supports menstrual regularity and detoxification.

Gokshura is another herb that supports both reproductive and urinary health. It is particularly useful in PCOS, as it improves ovarian function, clears excess Kapha, and reduces water retention. Manjistha, a blood purifier, is used to clear congestion in the artava srotas and improve skin health. Women with hormonal acne, fibroids, or endometriosis benefit from Manjistha's ability to gently cleanse and support circulation. Other supportive herbs include Nagkesar (to reduce bleeding), Jeera (to regulate digestion and hormones), and Vidari (to nourish reproductive tissue).

Ayurvedic wisdom does not stop at individual herbs—it has preserved complex, powerful formulations that synergize multiple herbs to amplify healing. *Churnas* (powders), *Asavas and Arishtas* (fermented tonics), and *Lehyas* (herbal jams or electuaries) are time-tested tools for systemic support.

Among churnas, *Triphala Churna* is perhaps the most well-known. Made of three fruits—Amalaki, Haritaki, and Bibhitaki—it balances all three doshas, supports detoxification, improves digestion, and enhances absorption. Its gentle effect on the colon has downstream benefits on hormonal balance, as proper elimination prevents toxin accumulation that would otherwise disrupt the endocrine system.

Asavas and Arishtas are self-fermented herbal preparations that penetrate deeply and work efficiently. *Ashokarishta*, as the name implies, is made from Ashoka and used for all types of menstrual irregularities. It is particularly helpful for women who feel emotionally depleted during menstruation, as it balances both physical symptoms and emotional heaviness. *Dashamoolarishta* is made from ten root herbs and is especially beneficial postpartum to help rebuild tissues, balance hormones, and restore energy. *Kumaryasava*, with Aloe Vera as its base, supports the liver, which plays a key role in hormone metabolism. Women with PCOS or sluggish digestion often benefit from it.

Lehyas are herbal confections made with jaggery, ghee, and sometimes milk. They are rich, heavy, and nourishing—ideal for building strength and vitality. *Chyawanprash*, the most popular Rasayana, includes Amalaki, Dashamoola, Ashwagandha, and over forty other herbs. It builds immunity, sharpens memory, supports respiratory health, and improves reproductive function. Taken daily with warm milk, it becomes a delicious and effective preventive. *Shatavari Kalpa*, a traditional formulation made from Shatavari root, sugar, and cardamom, is especially helpful during pregnancy, lactation, or menopause. *Drakshadi Lehyam*, made from grapes and herbs, cools the body, supports hemoglobin levels, and aids in recovery from fatigue.

These formulations are more than medicines—they are invitations to live in rhythm. They are not to be taken mindlessly, but with awareness. The act of preparing a tonic, the pause before drinking, the gentle rubbing of oil on the skin, the mindful chewing of an herbal jam—all become rituals of return. A return to slowness. A return to listening. A return to honoring the body as temple.

In the end, Ayurvedic herbs and Rasayana therapy do not treat diseases—they awaken health. They remind a woman that her vitality is not something she must earn, prove, or chase. It is already within her, waiting to be nourished, supported, and remembered. With every cup of herbal tea, every spoon of lehyam, every drop of medicated oil, she says to herself: "I am worth caring for." And it is in that simple act—repeated daily, lovingly, with devotion—that true healing begins.

Chapter 6: Panchakarma and Detox Therapies for Women

In the landscape of Ayurvedic healing, *Panchakarma* stands as a deeply revered practice—not merely a form of cleansing, but a profound journey of internal realignment, emotional reset, and spiritual refinement. It is a ritual of unburdening—of peeling away the layers of physical toxins, mental noise, and emotional residues that accumulate over time. For women, whose physiological and psychological experiences are intimately connected to rhythm and change, Panchakarma is not just beneficial—it is vital. It offers a sacred pause, a turning inward, and a return to one's essential self. Unlike modern detox trends that focus solely on calorie restriction or digestive flushes, Ayurveda approaches purification as a deeply personalized, cyclical, and nurturing process. It recognizes that true healing is not a war against the body, but an invitation to let go—with grace.

The modern woman, moving constantly between roles and expectations, often carries a unique blend of burden—nutritional deficiencies from hurried meals, adrenal fatigue from chronic stress, emotional heaviness from relational demands, and toxic load from cosmetics, pharmaceuticals, and processed food. In addition, societal pressures often teach her to suppress pain, ignore her body's cries, and power through discomfort. Over time, the body internalizes this suppression. The channels—the *srotas*—narrow. The tissues dry or congest. The digestion weakens. The mind becomes restless or dull. The monthly cycle becomes erratic or painful. Reproductive issues arise. Fatigue becomes chronic. Emotions begin to stagnate. And yet, amidst all this, the woman continues. She may not even realize how far she's drifted from her center until the symptoms become too loud to ignore.

This is where Panchakarma offers something extraordinary. It doesn't treat only the symptom. It doesn't ask the woman to mask her pain. Instead, it asks her to stop. To rest. To soften. To allow her body to finally release all that it's been holding. In its classical form, Panchakarma involves three stages—*Purva Karma* (preparation), *Pradhana Karma* (main therapies), and *Paschat Karma* (post-rejuvenation care). Each phase is sacred and essential, tailored to the woman's constitution, age, strength, imbalances, and life stage.

The preparatory phase, *Purva Karma*, includes Snehana (oleation) and Swedana (sudation). Oleation involves the internal and external application of oils—nourishing, penetrating, and loosening toxins embedded deep within the tissues. Daily oil massages using medicated oils such as *Dhanwantaram Taila* or *Balashwagandhadi Taila* calm the nervous system, soften Vata, and prepare the body to let go. Internally, medicated ghee (*Snehapana*) is consumed to liquefy lipid-soluble toxins and carry them back into the digestive tract for elimination. Swedana follows—herbal steam therapy that dilates channels, increases circulation, and encourages the movement of toxins outward.

During these days, the woman often begins to feel emotional waves—forgotten memories surfacing, fatigue emerging, unresolved grief presenting itself. Ayurveda embraces this as a natural part of the detox journey. What leaves through the skin, the colon, or the breath is not only physical—it is emotional memory. This is why the environment during Panchakarma is so important. A quiet, warm, safe, and supported space allows the woman to surrender to the healing process.

Then comes *Pradhana Karma*—the core Panchakarma therapies. For each woman, this is chosen carefully. A young woman with painful menstruation and constipation may need a series of Basti therapies. A perimenopausal woman with inflammatory skin issues may benefit from Virechana to purge excess Pitta. A postpartum woman suffering from Vata depletion may begin with nourishing internal *Snehana* before proceeding to *Matra Basti.*

Vamana, or therapeutic emesis, is rarely used in women except in strong Kapha conditions like obesity, hypothyroidism, or chronic congestion. It requires significant preparation and should only be done under close supervision. Virechana, on the other hand, is more commonly recommended. Administered after proper oleation and fasting, it flushes the small intestine and liver, removes excess Pitta, and has profound benefits for skin, hormones, bile regulation, and mental sharpness. It is often followed by a period of soft foods, rest, and gentle *Rasayana* therapies.

Basti, the enema therapy, is considered the most suitable and sacred Panchakarma treatment for women. Why? Because Vata is the primary force behind most women's disorders—whether it be menstrual pain, infertility, anxiety, premature aging, dryness, insomnia, or restlessness. Basti therapies directly pacify Vata by delivering herbal decoctions or oils into the colon—the seat of Vata. The colon is more than just a waste passage in Ayurveda—it is the doorway to the nervous system, reproductive system, and emotional body. With each *Anuvasana Basti* (oil-based), the body receives lubrication and grounding. With each *Niruha Basti* (decoction-based), toxins and excessive doshas are gently expelled.

Even a short 8-day or 15-day Basti protocol can profoundly change a woman's hormonal landscape, mood, bowel habits, and emotional resilience. For menopausal women, Basti therapies offer a smoother passage into the new rhythm of life. For menstruating women, they restore regularity, reduce PMS, and soothe uterine discomfort. For mothers, they offer repair, containment, and a sense of being held—something often denied in fast-paced postpartum recovery.

Nasya, the administration of medicated oils through the nostrils, works on the mind, sinuses, and hormonal axis. In women prone to PMS-related mood swings, anxiety, or migraines, Nasya clears the channels between the head and pelvis. *Anu Taila* is a classic oil used daily for lubrication and clarity. *Shadbindu Taila* is used in deeper detox protocols. *Brahmi Ghrita* or *Medhya Rasayana* formulations may be used in specific emotional or mental imbalances. The head is the gateway to consciousness, and Nasya gently opens this gate.

Raktamokshana, or bloodletting, is practiced less frequently today but holds value in specific cases. In women with chronic acne, endometriosis, or uterine congestion, blood purification through herbal support (using *Manjistha, Neem, Turmeric*) and dietary correction often suffices. Still, traditional techniques like leech therapy or needle pricking are sometimes used under trained practitioners to relieve local Pitta and stagnation.

After the main therapies, *Paschat Karma* begins. This post-treatment phase is where deep rejuvenation and rebuilding occur. The digestive fire is rekindled with *Samsarjana Krama*—a graduated diet beginning with rice gruel, *Kitchari*, and simple soups. Rasayana herbs like *Shatavari*, *Ashwagandha*, *Amalaki*, and *Bala* are introduced slowly to rebuild strength and tissue intelligence. Gentle yoga, meditation, breathwork, and journaling are recommended. The woman is encouraged to rest deeply, stay warm, avoid sensory overload, and reflect on what is no longer needed in her life.

Panchakarma is not a one-time event. It is a lifestyle. A commitment to returning to balance. Seasonal Panchakarma—especially during *Ritu Sandhi*, the junctions between seasons—becomes a rhythmic reset for the entire system. Women are deeply sensitive to seasonal and lunar shifts. Aligning Panchakarma with these natural transitions enhances its effect. For instance, a spring Panchakarma after the heaviness of winter helps eliminate excess Kapha, improve metabolism, and boost immunity. An autumn cleanse calms Pitta and Vata, preparing the body for the dry and cold months ahead.

Panchakarma can also be aligned with a woman's menstrual cycle. The ideal time for detox is post-menstruation, when the body is in a rebuilding phase. Detox during menstruation is contraindicated, as the body is already undergoing a natural release. Similarly, Panchakarma is not advised during pregnancy but is extremely helpful before conception and postpartum. For menopausal women, Panchakarma supports the transition into Vata-dominance and prevents common issues like osteoporosis, dryness, and cognitive decline.

Across cultures, traditions, and generations, women have sought ways to cleanse, retreat, and renew. Panchakarma is the embodied memory of those rituals—a structured, holistic, and intuitive system that recognizes that healing must touch every layer. In Ayurvedic clinics and hospitals, in home-based retreats and women's circles, countless stories emerge—stories of women who entered tired, lost, and disconnected, and emerged clear, radiant, and empowered. A young woman with fibroids finds herself pain-free after Panchakarma and a year of follow-up Rasayana. A mother with postpartum trauma discovers the joy of presence again. A woman at 50, sleepless and anxious, begins sleeping deeply, laughing easily, and feeling her life anew.

These stories are not miracles. They are what happens when the body is heard. When the mind is held. When the spirit is given space. Panchakarma is not simply about removing toxins—it is about removing what is not you. The heaviness. The noise. The fatigue. The shame. The patterns. What remains is clarity. Strength. Grace. Light.

And for the woman who walks this path, it is not just a treatment—it is a return. A remembering. A rebirth.

Chapter 7: Nutrition and Diet in Ayurveda for Women

In Ayurveda, food is not merely fuel—it is medicine, memory, and energy. It is a carrier of prana (life force), a builder of ojas (vitality), and a mirror of our mental and emotional state. For women, whose bodies and minds are attuned to cyclical rhythms, emotional tides, and hormonal flux, food holds a special kind of influence. Every meal has the potential to either balance or disturb, to nourish or exhaust. When a woman eats in alignment with her dosha, her digestive fire (agni), her reproductive stage, and the season, she not only maintains health—she glows. She moves with greater ease, rests more deeply, digests life more gently, and listens to herself more clearly. Ayurveda teaches that the quality of a woman's life begins with the quality of her digestion—not just of food, but of experiences, emotions, and energy.

At the heart of Ayurvedic nutrition lies the concept of a Sattvic diet—food that is pure, balanced, light, and infused with vitality. Sattva is the quality of clarity, harmony, and peace. It is the mental state associated with joy, compassion, and spiritual awareness. Sattvic foods are those that support these qualities. They include fresh vegetables, seasonal fruits, whole grains, ghee, soaked nuts and seeds, lentils, herbal teas, and gentle spices. These foods are not only easy to digest—they elevate the mind and stabilize emotions. They create a lightness in the body and a softness in the heart. Women who feel overwhelmed, anxious, heavy, or emotionally scattered often find that returning to a sattvic diet brings immediate relief—not only physically but emotionally.

Seasonal eating, or Ritucharya, is another pillar of Ayurvedic nutrition. Ayurveda recognizes that the qualities of each season interact with the doshas within us. In winter and early spring, Kapha accumulates, bringing heaviness, sluggishness, and mucus. This is the time for light, dry, and warming foods—barley, millet, ginger, mustard seeds, bitter greens, and lightly spiced soups. In summer, Pitta dominates with its heat and intensity. To pacify it, cooling foods like cucumber, coconut, rice, ghee, mint, fennel, and sweet fruits are emphasized. In autumn and early winter, Vata takes the lead, bringing dryness, cold, and unpredictability. During this time, women thrive on grounding foods—root vegetables, warm milk, sesame oil, oatmeal, soups, and stews spiced with cinnamon, cumin, and cardamom. Eating seasonally is not just a dietary habit—it is a way of dancing with nature. When a woman eats what nature offers, when it offers it, she feels held. She is reminded that nourishment is always available when she listens.

Just as the seasons change, so too does a woman's body across the arc of her life. Nutrition must evolve with these shifts. During adolescence, as Pitta and hormonal activity increase, the body needs building and cooling. Iron-rich foods, whole grains, greens, and sattvic proteins help establish regular cycles and emotional balance. Avoiding overly processed, spicy, and fried foods prevents Pitta from flaring into acne, mood swings, or irregular menstruation.

During the reproductive years, the body is in full rhythm. Nutrition during this stage focuses on maintaining ojas, supporting the menstrual cycle, and preparing for potential conception. Warm, cooked meals, nourishing fats like ghee and sesame oil, fresh vegetables, and proteins like mung dal or tofu help stabilize hormones and keep digestion strong. Spices like cumin, coriander, and fennel balance the digestive fire and reduce bloating. Herbs such as Shatavari, Guduchi, and Triphala are used regularly in teas or tonics to maintain equilibrium.

For women during pregnancy, food becomes even more sacred. She is not only feeding herself, but the consciousness growing within. Ayurveda prescribes a diet that is soft, warm, mildly spiced, and emotionally comforting. Ghee becomes central—nourishing the reproductive tissues, calming the nervous system, and aiding digestion. Warm milk with cardamom or saffron, rice, moong dal, stewed fruits, and gentle soups are staples. Rasayanas like Shatavari Kalpa and Drakshadi Lehyam are introduced based on trimester-specific needs. The diet is also infused with intention—the woman is encouraged to eat in a peaceful environment, to bless her food, and to be aware of how each meal nourishes both body and soul.

After childbirth, during the postpartum window, the focus shifts to Vata pacification. The woman's body is in a state of emptiness, vulnerability, and repair. Warmth, oiliness, and simplicity define the diet. Soupy rice gruels, ghee-laden dals, stewed carrots and beets, herbal teas with ginger and ajwain (carom seeds), and medicated ghee restore strength, digestion, and emotional stability. Cold, dry, and raw foods are avoided, as they aggravate Vata and can delay recovery.

In menopause, as the body transitions again and Vata increases, the diet must support moisture, bone strength, and emotional grounding. Foods that are warm, heavy, and slightly sweet in taste nourish shukra dhatu and ojas. Almond milk, sesame seeds, dates, root vegetables, ghee, cooked grains like amaranth or quinoa, and herbal tonics are all emphasized. Avoiding spicy, bitter, or overly dry foods helps reduce hot flashes, anxiety, and dryness. The woman is encouraged to eat slowly, without distraction, and to bring gratitude into each meal.

Even within these broader life stages, Ayurveda pays close attention to specific times in a woman's cycle—menstruation, ovulation, pregnancy, and menopause. During menstruation, the body is in a natural detoxification phase. The digestive fire is often lower, and the energy inward. This is not the time for heavy or stimulating foods. Light, warm meals such as soups, khichdi, herbal teas, and soft-cooked vegetables are ideal. Avoiding dairy, cold foods, refined sugars, and excessive caffeine helps reduce cramps, bloating, and mood swings. Herbal infusions with ginger, fennel, and cinnamon support flow and ease pain. Gentle self-care and mindful eating allow the body to cleanse fully and recover with grace.

During pregnancy, as previously noted, food becomes a medium of transmission—not just of nutrients, but of consciousness. Ayurveda encourages the woman to eat foods that are sattvic, easy to digest, and emotionally nurturing. She is advised to listen deeply to her cravings—not to indulge every one, but to inquire what she truly needs. A craving for sweets may signal a need for emotional comfort. A desire for sourness may reflect Pitta's rise. Through such awareness, she refines her diet not from a place of control but from connection.

In menopause, the emphasis shifts toward bone nourishment, mental clarity, and preserving ojas. This is the time to embrace nourishing routines—slow cooking, warm breakfasts, herbal infusions, and Rasayana therapy. Drinking warm water throughout the day, sipping milk with nutmeg at night, or having a spoonful of chyawanprash in the morning becomes a way of grounding the day. Meals are small, frequent, and lovingly prepared. The woman is reminded that she no longer needs to be everything for everyone—now, it is time to mother herself.

To support these practices, Ayurveda offers simple, delicious, and healing recipes. Kitchari, a one-pot meal made from mung dal and rice, is the cornerstone of Ayurvedic detox and nourishment. Cooked with ghee, cumin, turmeric, and ginger, it is easy to digest, deeply satisfying, and grounding. Variations can include seasonal vegetables, coconut milk, or chopped greens depending on the woman's dosha and stage of life.

Stewed apples with cinnamon make an excellent breakfast or snack for Vata and Pitta women. Laddus made from sesame seeds, jaggery, and ghee are wonderful for bone strength, especially in menopause. Warm milk with turmeric and saffron soothes the nervous system and promotes sleep. Teas made from fennel, cumin, and coriander support digestion. Ajwain and ginger teas relieve gas and cramping. Triphala at night ensures regular elimination, improving skin, sleep, and mood.

Ayurveda also uses kitchen herbs medicinally. Cumin, coriander, and fennel are the trio that balance digestion. Turmeric purifies the blood and supports the liver. Fenugreek supports lactation and reduces inflammation. Cardamom enhances digestion and calms the mind. These spices are not only flavor enhancers—they are daily tonics, woven into the fabric of meals to keep balance alive.

But more important than what is eaten is how it is eaten. Ayurveda teaches that the state of mind during meals is as important as the food itself. A rushed, distracted, or resentful meal—even if it is organic—will not nourish. A simple meal eaten with gratitude, presence, and joy becomes medicine. The woman is encouraged to eat in silence at least once a day, to chew slowly, to feel the warmth of the food, and to bow to the nourishment it brings.

Ultimately, Ayurvedic nutrition for women is not a set of restrictions—it is a path of remembrance. A remembrance that food is sacred. That the body is wise. That nourishment is not a task—it is a form of love. When a woman begins to eat in alignment with her constitution, her cycle, and the seasons, she does not only digest better—she lives better. She becomes more attuned to her emotions, more at peace with her body, more able to give without depletion. And in that state, she embodies what Ayurveda has always known: that health is not a goal to be chased, but a rhythm to be honored, every day, one meal at a time.

Chapter 8: Skin, Hair, and Beauty Care

In Ayurveda, beauty is not simply about appearance—it is the natural expression of inner harmony. True beauty radiates from a body that is balanced, a mind that is peaceful, and a soul that is nourished. Skin, hair, and external appearance are seen as reflections of deeper health, influenced by digestion, emotions, and lifestyle. For women, whose bodies are intricately tied to the cycles of nature and emotion, beauty is not a superficial quality but a sensitive indicator of well-being. Ayurveda honors this holistic vision by offering personalized skincare and haircare practices based on doshas, herbal wisdom, and seasonal self-care.

Ayurvedic skincare begins with understanding one's dosha constitution. Each dosha—Vata, Pitta, and Kapha—manifests distinct skin types and concerns. Vata skin is typically dry, thin, and prone to roughness and early aging. It benefits from deep hydration, oil-based therapies, and calming rituals. Pitta skin tends to be sensitive, fair, and prone to inflammation, redness, and acne. It requires cooling, soothing, and anti-inflammatory care. Kapha skin is thick, oily, and resilient but may be prone to congestion, enlarged pores, and dullness. It needs stimulation, detoxification, and light, drying herbs and scrubs. The Ayurvedic view encourages not just treating the skin topically but harmonizing the internal doshic balance through diet, lifestyle, and emotional awareness.

For Vata skin, oils like sesame, almond, or avocado are recommended. Daily self-massage with warm oil (abhyanga), followed by a gentle herbal cleanser with rose, chamomile, or oat flour, nourishes and protects. Masks made of ripe banana, honey, and a pinch of ashwagandha powder restore softness. Incorporating cooked foods, warm herbal teas, and spices like cinnamon and cardamom can also support Vata from within. Pitta skin benefits from aloe vera gel, rose water, sandalwood, and neem. A face mask made of fuller's earth, turmeric, and cucumber juice helps reduce redness and inflammation. Internal cooling through foods like cilantro, coconut water, and fresh pomegranate further supports skin health. For Kapha skin, gentle exfoliation using chickpea flour, turmeric, and yogurt is ideal. Ubtans (herbal scrubs) with tulsi, mint, and a pinch of black pepper stimulate circulation and clear clogged pores. Spices like ginger, mustard seed, and clove are used to invigorate digestion and reduce Kapha's sluggishness.

Hair care in Ayurveda is similarly dosha-based. Vata hair is dry, brittle, and frizzy. It needs oiling with warm sesame or bhringraj oil, nourishing hair masks with yogurt, hibiscus, and aloe vera, and gentle scalp massage to stimulate growth. Internally, hydration, nourishing fats, and calming herbs like Brahmi and Shatavari are used. Pitta hair tends to be fine and prone to early graying or hair loss. Cooling oils like coconut, amla, and brahmi are beneficial, along with gentle shampoos made from shikakai or reetha. Adding bitter and sweet tastes in the diet, reducing heat-producing foods, and practicing mental calm support Pitta balance. Kapha hair is thick and oily and may experience heaviness or dandruff. Regular cleansing with light, astringent herbs like neem and fenugreek, and dry herbal powders, helps maintain scalp health. Light eating patterns, dry brushing, and stimulating herbs like guggulu help prevent Kapha accumulation.

Beyond individual treatments, Ayurveda emphasizes natural beauty rituals that purify the body and enhance glow from within. Daily routines such as tongue scraping, oil pulling, abhyanga (self-massage), and warm baths infused with herbs not only support skin but also detoxify the lymphatic system and calm the nervous system. Herbal steaming with rose petals, tulsi, or lavender opens pores and infuses skin with prana. Facial massage using oils or ghee nourishes facial tissues, reduces wrinkles, and brings softness. Weekly masks and scrubs remove dead skin and renew the complexion. Incorporating breathing techniques like Nadi Shodhana and meditation enhances internal harmony, making the outer radiance more pronounced.

Detox plays a vital role in maintaining natural beauty. When ama (toxins) accumulates due to poor digestion, stress, or environmental factors, it shows up as dull skin, acne, pigmentation, or hair issues. Ayurvedic detox involves light, seasonal diets, gentle fasting, warm water, digestive teas (cumin-coriander-fennel), Triphala, and Panchakarma when needed. Skin-specific herbal blood purifiers such as manjistha, neem, guduchi, and turmeric are often used to clear heat and stagnation from the body, promoting clarity and radiance. Supporting elimination through proper hydration, fiber intake, and regular sleep cycles ensures that detoxification channels stay open and effective.

Daily beauty regimens in Ayurveda are simple yet profoundly transformative. Morning routines begin with cleansing the face with cool water, misting with rose or vetiver hydrosol, applying herbal serum or oil suited to dosha, and gently massaging the face to awaken the skin.

Weekly beauty regimens may include full-body oil massage, exfoliating scrubs, herbal face packs, and scalp treatments. Seasonal beauty routines align with Ritucharya. In spring, detoxifying scrubs and light oils balance Kapha. In summer, cooling masks and rosewater soothe Pitta. In autumn and winter, deeply moisturizing rituals protect against Vata's drying effects. Traditional ingredients like saffron, milk, and sandalwood are used across seasons to enhance glow and even skin tone.

Additionally, Ayurveda places great importance on emotional beauty. A joyful, peaceful, and kind mind reflects as softness in features, warmth in the eyes, and calmness in expression. Unprocessed emotions like anger, grief, and fear can manifest physically as frown lines, jaw tension, or skin outbreaks. Regular self-reflection, emotional journaling, and spiritual practices like mantra chanting or prayer help maintain emotional clarity. Beauty, therefore, is not applied—it is cultivated. Cultivated through awareness, intentional rituals, and a reverent relationship with nature.

Ultimately, Ayurvedic beauty is about honoring the body as a temple. When a woman cares for her skin and hair with love, presence, and intention, her inner radiance naturally reflects in her outer glow. It is not about perfection, but about presence. Ayurveda invites her not to chase beauty but to remember that she already is it—and that through balance, care, and nature's grace, her light can shine effortlessly.

Chapter 9: Daily and Seasonal Regimens (Dinacharya & Ritucharya)

n Ayurveda, health is not a static condition to be maintained through rigid control, but a dynamic dance with the rhythms of the natural world. This philosophy extends beyond medicine into the daily and seasonal flow of life, known as *Dinacharya* (daily regimen) and *Ritucharya* (seasonal regimen). These two concepts form the foundation for aligning the individual body with the cosmic order, ensuring balance between inner and outer environments. For women, whose biological systems are intimately tied to cycles—of the moon, of the menstrual flow, of reproduction, and of emotion—these regimens are not only beneficial, but essential. They provide a framework for cultivating groundedness, vitality, mental clarity, and emotional equanimity.

Dinacharya, the Ayurvedic daily routine, is a blueprint for living in tune with the natural rise and fall of the sun, the body's internal clock, and the movement of the doshas throughout the day. Rather than being a set of restrictive habits, Dinacharya invites a woman into a nurturing ritual of self-care, attentiveness, and respect for her body and its needs. It begins even before the sun rises, during the *Brahma Muhurta*, a sacred window approximately 90 minutes before sunrise. This time is considered especially sattvic—infused with purity, peace, and clarity—and is ideal for meditation, reflection, breathwork, or journaling. Rising at this time helps align the body's natural circadian rhythm, enhancing immunity, digestion, and mental focus.

The first act upon waking is cleansing—both literal and energetic. Washing the face, eyes, and mouth with cool water clears the senses. Tongue scraping removes ama that accumulates overnight and provides insight into the body's inner condition. Oil pulling with sesame or coconut oil detoxifies the oral cavity and strengthens the gums. Drinking a glass of warm water with lemon or herbal infusions flushes the digestive tract and signals the body that it is time to awaken.

Elimination follows, and a regular bowel movement is considered one of the key signs of health in Ayurveda. Women with erratic digestion, sluggish bowels, or bloating are encouraged to gently stimulate elimination through warm water, Triphala at night, or castor oil under guidance. This is followed by self-massage or *Abhyanga*, using warm oil suited to the dosha. Vata women benefit from sesame oil, Pitta from coconut or sunflower oil, and Kapha from mustard or dry powder massage (*Udvartana*). This ritual is not merely cosmetic—it nourishes the skin, calms the nervous system, enhances lymphatic flow, and provides a grounding sense of embodiment.

After oiling, bathing in warm water cleanses the body and invigorates the senses. Natural cleansers like green gram flour, sandalwood paste, or rose petal powder may be used in place of harsh soaps. Women are encouraged to wear clean, comfortable clothing, apply a small amount of oil to the crown of the head and soles of the feet, and enter the day with calm intention. Morning meals are ideally light and nourishing, such as spiced oatmeal, stewed apples, or rice gruel. Food should be eaten mindfully, seated, and without distraction.

Throughout the day, Ayurveda recommends pacing activity to correspond with the movement of doshas. From sunrise to mid-morning, Kapha predominates, making this the best time for physical exercise. Brisk walking, yoga, sun salutations, or dance can stimulate circulation and counteract Kapha's heaviness. From mid-morning to mid-afternoon, Pitta governs digestion, focus, and energy, making this the optimal window for the main meal, work, or creative pursuits. Meals should be warm, well-spiced, and satisfying but not excessive. Cold, raw, or heavy foods should be avoided as they dull agni.

The afternoon into evening marks the return of Vata—a time of creativity, reflection, and gentle winding down. Evening meals should be smaller, lighter, and eaten at least two hours before sleep. Herbal teas with ginger, fennel, or chamomile soothe digestion and prepare the mind for rest. Electronic stimulation, intense conversation, or emotional drama should be minimized. A soothing evening routine may include a warm bath, light oil massage, journaling, prayer, or gentle breathing practices.

Sleep is sacred in Ayurveda. Women, particularly those with Vata imbalances, must protect their rest. Bedtime ideally falls between 9:30 and 10:00 PM to ensure alignment with the natural energy descent that begins after sunset. Sleep is not merely physical recovery—it is when the mind digests impressions, the tissues repair, and the nervous system recalibrates. Women suffering from insomnia, anxious thoughts, or hormonal restlessness can benefit from herbal support such as Brahmi, Ashwagandha, or Jatamansi, and from sleep rituals like warm milk with nutmeg, meditation, or cooling foot massage.

While Dinacharya offers a stable daily rhythm, *Ritucharya* introduces the art of seasonal living. Ayurveda divides the year into six seasons, each with its own predominant doshic energy. Aligning lifestyle, diet, and activity with these rhythms prevents seasonal diseases, supports digestion, and protects ojas. In spring (*Vasanta*), Kapha increases and the body begins to detoxify naturally. This is the season for cleansing—light meals, bitter greens, herbal teas, and dry brushing help eliminate excess Kapha. In summer (*Grishma*), Pitta dominates and the body is more prone to heat, dehydration, and inflammation. Cooling foods like cucumbers, melons, rose water, ghee, and coconut water soothe Pitta, while avoiding overexertion protects strength.

Monsoon season (*Varsha*) is marked by dampness, weakened digestion, and Vata-Pitta imbalances. Steamed vegetables, sour tastes, ginger tea, and digestive spices help stabilize agni. Autumn (*Sharad*) is the season of Pitta again, and like summer, it requires cooling herbs and foods, emotional balance, and skin care. Early winter (*Hemanta*) brings strength, higher appetite, and Kapha-Vata tendencies. This is the time to nourish with ghee, warm grains, root vegetables, soups, and Rasayana herbs. Late winter (*Shishira*) continues this trend, though the cold intensifies. Physical activity is encouraged, and Rasayanas like Chyawanprash build ojas.

For women, Ritucharya becomes especially potent when synchronized with the menstrual cycle. Just as nature has periods of expansion and withdrawal, the body undergoes similar transitions. Menstruation is a time of release and rest. Ovulation is a time of radiance and creation. Premenstrual days are best for introspection. Ayurveda advises women to live in rhythm with their own bodies, allowing rest during menstruation, nourishment during ovulation, and purification during late luteal phases. Herbal teas, warm oil massages, moon bathing, and gentle yoga can be tailored to each phase.

Ritucharya also influences emotional health. Seasonal affective tendencies—such as anxiety in autumn, lethargy in spring, or irritability in summer—can be soothed through appropriate seasonal adjustments. Clothing, sleep times, work pace, and even social interactions are best aligned with the energy of the season. For example, winter is ideal for reflection and solitude, while summer invites connection and celebration.

In this way, Dinacharya and Ritucharya are not just schedules—they are philosophies. They invite a woman to live with awareness, to respect the tides of nature, and to build her health not through force but through flow. Through daily attention to self-care and seasonal wisdom, she cultivates resilience, grace, and inner radiance. Ayurveda reminds her that she is not separate from nature—she is nature. And in aligning with the sun, the moon, the wind, and the rain, she returns home to herself.

This is the essence of Ayurvedic living: not a rigid protocol, but a sacred rhythm. Not a list of things to do, but a way of being. When a woman embraces Dinacharya and Ritucharya with devotion, she no longer lives in opposition to her body or the world around her. She dances with them. She flows. And in that flow, health is not something she chases—it is something she naturally becomes.

Chapter 10: Yoga, Meditation, and Mental Well-being

In the Ayurvedic tradition, the mind is not separate from the body, and mental health is not separate from physical wellness. The ancient seers understood that true healing must encompass both dimensions—to bring balance to the body while cultivating peace in the mind. It is from this holistic understanding that the practices of Yoga and Ayurveda evolved as sister sciences. Where Ayurveda provides the framework for physical health and constitutional balance, Yoga offers the tools for mental clarity, emotional regulation, and spiritual integration. For women, whose lives are marked by constant change—biologically, emotionally, and socially—Yoga and meditation serve as anchors, offering inner steadiness amidst outer turbulence. This chapter explores how these practices, when thoughtfully integrated with Ayurvedic wisdom, become powerful allies in promoting hormonal harmony, emotional balance, and lasting mental well-being.

Asanas, or physical postures in Yoga, serve more than a physical purpose. When chosen and practiced mindfully, they directly influence the hormonal system, calm the nervous system, and create space for emotional release. For hormonal balance, especially in cases of PMS, PCOS, menopause, or adrenal fatigue, gentle, restorative postures are ideal. Asanas like Supta Baddha Konasana (Reclining Bound Angle Pose), Viparita Karani (Legs Up the Wall), Setu Bandhasana (Bridge Pose), and Balasana (Child's Pose) help regulate the endocrine glands and soothe the mind. Twisting poses, when practiced carefully, massage the abdominal organs and support detoxification, improving digestive and reproductive function. Regular practice of forward bends, like Paschimottanasana (Seated Forward Fold), calms Pitta and Vata, easing anxiety and irritability. Heart-opening poses, such as Bhujangasana (Cobra) or Ustrasana (Camel Pose), stimulate the thymus and heart chakra, encouraging emotional release and compassion.

It is not only the pose that heals, but the attitude with which it is performed. A woman practicing asana in a state of self-judgment or perfectionism may intensify her imbalance. But when she moves with breath, awareness, and acceptance, her yoga becomes medicine. A slow, conscious practice—even if short in duration—has the power to restore balance far more effectively than a strenuous routine performed without awareness. Ayurveda suggests adapting asana practice to the time of day, season, and individual constitution. Vata women should favor grounding, stabilizing postures with longer holds. Pitta women benefit from cooling, non-competitive sequences. Kapha types thrive on stimulating, invigorating flows that counteract lethargy.

The practice of asanas for mental health is further enhanced when interwoven with chanting or sound. Vibrational energy through sound and breath penetrates deeply into the subtle body. The repetition of mantras such as "Om," "So Hum," or seed sounds like "Lam," "Yam," and "Sham" in coordination with postures further awakens dormant energy and purifies emotional stagnation. In Yoga therapy, sequences are often designed to harmonize with a woman's cycle, emotional needs, and Ayurvedic constitution. Yin

Yoga and Yoga Nidra have also gained importance as forms that activate parasympathetic relaxation and deep cellular repair.

Breath, or prana, is the bridge between body and mind. Through *Pranayama*, the practice of breath regulation, women can access deep reservoirs of calm, clarity, and vitality. Pranayama not only enhances oxygenation and lung capacity but also directly affects the nervous system and endocrine function. For stress relief and emotional balance, Nadi Shodhana (Alternate Nostril Breathing) is among the most effective techniques. It balances the left and right hemispheres of the brain, calms Vata, and harmonizes the nervous system. Bhramari (Humming Bee Breath) soothes anxiety, improves sleep, and balances thyroid function. Ujjayi (Victorious Breath), practiced with awareness, warms the body, improves concentration, and helps regulate emotions in stressful environments.

For Pitta-related imbalances such as anger, frustration, or hot flashes, Sheetali and Sheetkari (cooling breaths) are ideal. These techniques reduce internal heat and promote emotional cooling. For Kapha tendencies like depression, heaviness, or sluggishness, energizing practices like Bhastrika (Bellows Breath) or Kapalabhati (Skull-Shining Breath) awaken the mind and stimulate metabolic fire. As with asana, pranayama should be practiced according to individual constitution, current imbalances, and life stage. During menstruation or pregnancy, gentler techniques are advised. All breathwork should be practiced on an empty stomach and in a quiet, well-ventilated space.

Consistent pranayama transforms not just breath patterns but the very way a woman experiences time, space, and tension. A woman who consciously breathes finds that she is more patient, less reactive, and more attuned to herself and her environment. Her breath becomes a friend—one that steadies her through grief, grounds her through stress, and uplifts her through fatigue.

Meditation, the art of inner stillness, completes the triad of Yoga practice. For women, whose thoughts may run in many directions, and whose emotional sensitivity is both a gift and a challenge, meditation provides sanctuary. It is the practice of turning inward—of resting in the silence beneath the noise, of observing rather than reacting, of reconnecting with one's true nature. Regular meditation has been shown to reduce cortisol, improve sleep, balance mood, enhance memory, and foster emotional resilience. But beyond these benefits, it reconnects a woman with her inner wisdom, allowing her to make choices from clarity rather than compulsion.

Meditation does not require a particular posture or belief system. It begins with awareness—of the breath, of sensations, of thoughts. Simple practices such as breath observation, mantra repetition (like "So Hum" or "Om Shanti"), or guided visualizations can be powerful tools. Women who struggle with emotional overwhelm may find relief in heart-based meditations, focusing on love, forgiveness, or compassion. Those navigating grief or change may benefit from grounding meditations, visualizing roots growing into the earth. Even five minutes of stillness, when practiced consistently, can shift the trajectory of one's day.

Advanced meditation practices such as Yoga Nidra—a guided form of conscious relaxation—are especially useful for women suffering from chronic fatigue, trauma, or insomnia. This deeply restorative technique guides the practitioner into a state between wakefulness and sleep, allowing for nervous system reset and emotional integration. Trataka, or candle gazing, enhances concentration, supports eye health, and calms mental restlessness. Japa meditation, involving the repetition of a mantra with the aid of a mala (rosary), is a deeply devotional practice that connects mind, body, and spirit.

Integrating Yoga and Ayurveda offers a holistic path to well-being that is responsive, intuitive, and sustainable. Ayurveda informs when, how, and what type of yoga to practice based on one's dosha, digestion, season, and cycle. It teaches that a Vata-dominant woman in autumn may need restorative yoga and warm oil massage, while a Pitta woman in summer may need moon salutations, coconut water, and meditation by candlelight. A Kapha woman in spring may benefit from dynamic sun salutations, dry brushing, and invigorating breathwork. When Yoga is practiced through the Ayurvedic lens, it ceases to be a generic exercise and becomes a deeply personal ritual of balance and self-awareness.

Moreover, the integration of these sciences supports every stage of a woman's life. In adolescence, yoga builds confidence and body awareness. In the reproductive years, it supports fertility, emotional stability, and stress resilience. During pregnancy, prenatal yoga enhances connection to the baby and prepares the body for labor. Postpartum, gentle yoga restores strength and calms the mind. In menopause, yoga provides grounding, emotional ease, and hormonal support. Throughout life, meditation anchors the spirit and affirms one's inner truth.

Ultimately, the practices of yoga, pranayama, and meditation are not separate from Ayurveda—they are its extensions. They take the principles of balance, rhythm, and self-care and embody them in movement, breath, and stillness. For the modern woman, whose life may be marked by urgency, complexity, and fragmentation, these practices offer coherence. They are reminders that peace is not found in external perfection but in internal presence. That health is not a static goal but a dynamic relationship with self. And that in returning to the breath, to the mat, and to silence, she returns to her own sacred wholeness. When she steps onto her mat with devotion, breathes with intention, and sits in stillness with awareness, she is not only healing—she is remembering who she is.

Chapter 11: Integrating Ayurveda in Modern Life

In an age defined by urgency, overstimulation, and digital overload, the ancient wisdom of Ayurveda may appear to be a relic of the past. But this science, rooted in observation of nature and rhythm, is not only timeless—it is more relevant today than ever. The fast-paced, convenience-driven modern world often pulls individuals away from their bodies, their intuition, and their sense of inner calm. Ayurveda, with its emphasis on balance, routine, and self-awareness, offers a profound antidote. Rather than demanding a complete lifestyle overhaul, it integrates seamlessly into daily life through small but meaningful rituals. For modern women—juggling roles, expectations, and self-care—Ayurveda provides a nurturing path back to self.

The core principle of Ayurveda is living in alignment with nature. In today's world, that often means learning how to slow down, how to listen, and how to prioritize what truly sustains health. Ayurveda does not insist on perfection; it encourages presence. A woman who wakes five minutes earlier to sit in silence, who chooses warm water over iced coffee, who eats mindfully instead of while scrolling a screen—she is practicing Ayurveda. These simple shifts help bring awareness to how modern life may be disrupting digestion, sleep, mood, and energy. This awareness is not passive—it is transformative. It creates a spaciousness in the mind, a softness in the body, and a renewed connection to inner wisdom.

Modern living often comes with erratic schedules, travel, emotional strain, and exposure to processed foods and pollutants. Ayurveda recognizes this and offers grounding tools to build resilience. Daily routines, or *Dinacharya*, are at the heart of modern Ayurvedic practice. Starting the day with tongue scraping, warm water, self-massage with oil, and a moment of gratitude creates a buffer against chaos. Simple food habits—eating warm meals, avoiding late-night snacks, chewing thoroughly—enhance digestion and mental clarity. Even five minutes of breath awareness, a cup of herbal tea, or a walk in nature restores a sense of control and connection.

For working women especially, Ayurveda emphasizes sustainable self-care. Long hours, screen fatigue, decision fatigue, and multitasking take a toll on the nervous system and hormonal health. Integrating Ayurveda into the workday can be as simple as stepping away from the screen to eat lunch mindfully, sipping cumin-coriander-fennel tea between meetings, or rubbing warm oil on the feet before bed. Creating boundaries—digital and energetic—is also Ayurvedic. Saying no to overstimulation, curating what is consumed visually and emotionally, and honoring the body's signals are all part of holistic living. Small habits like keeping a bottle of rose water for facial spritzing during long work sessions or stretching gently between tasks can make a world of difference.

The Ayurvedic concept of *sattva* (mental clarity and peace) is particularly powerful for modern women. In a culture that often rewards hustle and productivity, Ayurveda honors rest, softness, and inner listening. Activities that promote sattva include journaling, meditation, volunteering, cooking, gardening, or simply spending time in stillness. Rather than compartmentalizing wellness into the weekends or holidays, Ayurveda encourages women to weave small acts of nourishment into daily life. Lighting a candle before meals, blessing the food, or offering a few moments of silence before sleeping can become anchors of calm amidst chaos.

Women often report that once they begin adopting Ayurvedic practices—even in small doses—they start noticing profound changes. Energy levels improve, mood becomes more stable, digestion becomes smoother, and sleep deepens. But even more significant is the shift in self-relationship. Ayurveda cultivates self-trust. A woman learns to hear her hunger cues, to feel when she needs rest, to recognize when something is too much. Her decisions start aligning with her intuition. She begins to experience her body not as a burden but as a wise guide.

Ayurveda is not a one-size-fits-all model. Its beauty lies in its adaptability. A woman living in a city with a hectic commute may need a different rhythm than one working remotely in a quiet town. A breastfeeding mother has different needs than a post-menopausal artist. Ayurveda honors these distinctions. It gives women permission to adapt, to experiment, and to evolve. It offers the principle of *pragya aparadha*—the "mistake of the intellect"—as the root of imbalance, and teaches how returning to inner wisdom heals that mistake.

Case studies further highlight the transformative power of integrating Ayurveda into modern living. One woman, a marketing executive with irregular periods and insomnia, began a basic routine of morning oil massage, warm spiced breakfast, and nightly Brahmi tea. Within two months, her cycle regularized, and she reported better sleep and focus. Another story comes from a mother of two who suffered from burnout and digestive issues. By switching from cold salads to cooked grains and vegetables, setting a regular meal time, and practicing alternate nostril breathing each evening, her energy and digestion improved dramatically.

A freelance artist navigating anxiety and creativity blocks found grounding in Vata-pacifying rituals: sesame oil massage, consistent sleep, and pranayama. These seemingly minor changes opened a deeper sense of self-trust and creative flow. A teacher dealing with hormonal imbalances during perimenopause found relief through Shatavari tea, sun salutations, and a simplified, seasonal diet. A tech entrepreneur learned to manage her migraines with weekly abhyanga, daily ginger-turmeric tea, and digital detox evenings. Each of these stories reflects a key truth: Ayurveda meets women where they are.

For women navigating transitions—whether pregnancy, postpartum, menopause, or emotional upheaval—Ayurveda becomes an invaluable companion. During pregnancy, women are encouraged to eat warm, nourishing foods, receive oil massages, rest deeply, and engage in sattvic practices like chanting or gratitude journaling. Postpartum care emphasizes Vata pacification, rest, and simple rituals. In menopause, the emphasis shifts to cooling foods, grounding yoga, and herbs like Shatavari and Ashoka.

Ayurveda provides a roadmap for these life passages, affirming that each phase is sacred and deserving of care.

The beauty of Ayurveda lies in its flexibility. It does not ask women to give up their careers, ambitions, or lifestyle preferences. It simply asks them to return to what feels natural, nourishing, and wise. In doing so, it reawakens the body's own healing intelligence. It reminds women that health is not found in external formulas but in internal rhythm. And it assures them that even in a fast-paced world, it is possible to live slowly, consciously, and beautifully.

Ayurvedic integration can also be supported through technology. Mindful use of apps for breathwork, yoga, or sleep tracking can enhance routine without dominating it. Creating a digital Ayurvedic journal or tracking doshic shifts during the menstrual cycle can be both educational and empowering. Women can also create community through online support circles, cooking groups, or seasonal cleansing retreats. Ayurveda is about connection—to self, to others, and to the earth.

In essence, Ayurveda in the modern world is not about ancient rituals locked in time. It is about remembering how to live with awareness, with breath, and with love. Whether in a corporate office, a bustling kitchen, or a quiet room at night, Ayurveda is there—guiding, supporting, and restoring balance one choice at a time. It is not the loudest voice, but it is the steadiest. And for the modern woman, it is the most loyal companion on the journey to self-knowing, self-healing, and radiant living.

Chapter 12: Fertility and Conception in Ayurveda

Fertility, in the Ayurvedic tradition, is not merely a biological function but a sacred process governed by balance, rhythm, purity, and intention. It is deeply intertwined with the laws of nature, cosmic harmony, and personal well-being. Ayurveda does not see conception as a mechanical union of sperm and ovum but as a profound convergence of body, mind, and soul—an opportunity to bring a new life imbued with vitality, clarity, and emotional strength into the world. In this context, the journey toward fertility and conception is not simply a path of reproduction but one of purification, rejuvenation, self-awareness, and preparation on all levels.

The Ayurvedic perspective emphasizes that the creation of a healthy and conscious child depends on four fundamental factors: Ritu (the proper time for conception), Kshetra (the health and preparedness of the reproductive organs), Ambu (the nutrition and fluid balance supporting reproduction), and Beeja (the health and vitality of the sperm and ovum). Each of these elements must be in balance, just as fertile soil, the right season, adequate water, and a strong seed are required to grow a flourishing plant. Conception is a natural result when these factors harmonize. But in modern times, many of these variables have been disturbed due to lifestyle disorders, emotional imbalances, over-medication, environmental toxins, irregular routines, poor diets, and chronic stress. Ayurveda seeks to correct these imbalances through individualized treatment, purification therapies, nutrition, and deep emotional healing.

In women, the readiness for conception is linked to the purity and strength of Artava, the reproductive tissue responsible for ovulation and the menstrual cycle. A regular, painless, and rhythmically flowing menstrual cycle is seen as an indicator of reproductive health. When this cycle is disturbed—whether by hormonal imbalances, improper digestion, emotional trauma, or doshic aggravations—the body's capacity to conceive naturally diminishes. Similarly, the uterus must be free of blockages, inflammation, or congestion for successful implantation to occur. Ayurveda pays meticulous attention to these details by ensuring that the body is not only free from disease but is in a state of optimal nourishment and clarity.

A cornerstone of Ayurvedic fertility planning is the process of Shodhana, or bodily purification. Before attempting conception, both partners are advised to undergo a thorough detoxification of their systems. This is because the buildup of Ama—undigested toxins—can obstruct the Srotas, or subtle body channels, preventing the proper movement of nutrients, hormones, and reproductive energy. Shodhana includes Panchakarma therapies such as Vamana (therapeutic emesis), Virechana (purgation), Basti (medicated enemas), and Nasya (nasal detox). These treatments are customized based on an individual's constitution, current imbalances, and lifestyle. For women, specific procedures like Uttara Basti—a medicated enema administered directly into the uterus—are especially beneficial for conditions such as uterine fibroids, tubal blockages, endometriosis, and unexplained infertility. After purification, the body enters a phase of rejuvenation through Rasayana therapies, which rebuild tissues, restore vitality, and support the deeper layers of reproductive functioning.

Ayurveda places a high value on the preparatory stage before conception, a phase that can span several weeks or months. During this time, the body is nurtured through proper diet, lifestyle, and emotional balance. Daily routines are aligned with nature—waking before sunrise, practicing self-massage, doing gentle yoga or walking, consuming freshly cooked meals, avoiding stale and processed foods, and sleeping by 10 p.m. are foundational practices. Food becomes medicine during this phase. Sattvic, warm, and easily digestible meals are emphasized. Cooked vegetables, whole grains, ghee, seasonal fruits, and digestive spices like cumin, fennel, ginger, and turmeric are encouraged. Fermented, fried, overly spicy, or cold foods are discouraged as they disrupt Agni, the digestive fire, and may lead to toxin accumulation. Regular bowel movements, clear skin, lightness of body, and a calm mind are seen as signs that the body is prepared.

Herbs play an essential role in supporting fertility. Shatavari, revered as the queen of herbs for women, nourishes the womb, enhances ovulation, and stabilizes hormonal fluctuations. Its cooling, moistening, and building properties make it particularly useful for Vata and Pitta imbalances. Ashwagandha is another cornerstone herb, often used for its grounding, restorative, and adaptogenic properties. It enhances libido, reduces stress, and improves sperm quality in men. Lodhra is beneficial for uterine toning, especially in conditions where the uterus is lax or prone to heavy bleeding. Kapikacchu is used to increase dopamine levels and improve male reproductive functions, while Gokshura is known to regulate hormones and support overall urogenital health in both sexes. These herbs are commonly administered in the form of churnas (powders), lehyas (herbal jams), asavas (fermented liquids), and ghritas (medicated ghee). Notable among these is Phala Ghrita, a traditional formulation used to enhance fertility and support uterine strength.

The role of male fertility is given equal importance in Ayurveda. Shukra dhatu, the reproductive tissue in men, is not only responsible for sperm production but also closely related to vitality, immunity, and emotional resilience. The health of Shukra depends on the health of all preceding dhatus—from Rasa (plasma) to Majja (bone marrow)—as each tissue layer nourishes the next. Factors such as excessive sexual activity, overwork, stress, alcohol, smoking, and late nights deplete Shukra, leading to conditions like low sperm count, poor motility, or erectile dysfunction. Men are therefore advised to follow a similar preparatory regimen, including Panchakarma, Rasayana therapy, nourishing diet, and lifestyle discipline. In many cases, both partners are treated simultaneously to ensure that the seed and the soil are in perfect harmony.

Another profound layer of Ayurvedic fertility care involves emotional and psychological readiness. Ayurveda recognizes that unresolved traumas, grief, suppressed anger, chronic anxiety, and relational conflict can block conception. Emotional toxins are considered just as detrimental as physical ones. Practices like Abhyanga (self-massage), Shirodhara (oil stream on the forehead), Nasya (nasal oil therapy), and meditation help to pacify the mind, regulate the nervous system, and create a deep sense of calm. Women are especially encouraged to connect with their creative energies, establish inner stillness, and cultivate joy and receptivity during this phase. Relationship harmony is vital; the emotional environment between partners at the time of conception is believed to imprint itself upon the developing fetus.

Ayurveda also describes the timing of conception with great sensitivity. The most fertile days are counted from the onset of menstruation, with ovulation occurring around the 12th to 16th day for women with a 28–30-day cycle. However, Ayurveda does not only emphasize physiological timing but also considers the quality of time, or Kaala. Certain lunar phases, planetary alignments, and times of day are considered more auspicious for conception. While such considerations may seem esoteric, they reflect a holistic worldview where all aspects of life—physical, mental, spiritual, and cosmic—are interconnected.

Garbha Samskara, the Ayurvedic philosophy of conscious conception and prenatal education, begins at the moment of thought or desire to bring a child into the world. This process involves purifying the body, mind, and soul to offer the highest quality environment for the incoming soul. Reciting mantras, reading sacred texts, engaging in acts of compassion, and maintaining inner peace are all part of this preparation. These practices elevate the vibration of both parents and are believed to influence not just physical health but the emotional and spiritual blueprint of the child.

Infertility, or Vandhyatva, in Ayurvedic diagnosis is not viewed as a standalone disease but as a symptom of underlying doshic imbalance. It may arise from Vata disturbances causing dryness and depletion, Pitta imbalances leading to inflammation and hormonal disruptions, or Kapha blockages that create sluggishness, cysts, or congestion. Each condition is approached uniquely, with customized herbs, therapies, and lifestyle prescriptions. For example, PCOS—a common cause of infertility—is often treated by reducing Kapha, improving insulin metabolism, and regularizing menstrual cycles through warming, stimulating herbs and appropriate detox. Endometriosis may require deeper cleansing, emotional healing, and surgical guidance in conjunction with Ayurveda.

Importantly, Ayurveda honors the dignity of the fertility journey, recognizing that not every woman may conceive in the same timeframe or manner. The focus is not on mechanical reproduction but on preparing oneself fully—physically, emotionally, spiritually—for the possibility of new life. If pregnancy does not occur, the Ayurvedic approach gently redirects the individual's energy toward creative, nurturing paths that may also fulfill the maternal instinct, such as caring for others, artistic expression, or healing service.

In the fast-paced world of modern fertility treatments—often filled with invasive diagnostics, synthetic hormones, and emotional rollercoasters—Ayurveda offers a slower, more conscious, and profoundly empowering path. It invites the individual to step into alignment with the rhythms of nature, to see conception not as a clinical event but as a sacred transition, and to become an active participant in the creation of life with full awareness and grace. This is perhaps the greatest gift Ayurveda offers: the reawakening of reverence for life, in its most delicate and divine expression.

Through the Ayurvedic path to fertility and conception, a woman does not merely prepare to birth a child—she prepares to birth a higher version of herself, deeply rooted in nature, aligned with truth, and open to receiving the miracle of life with gratitude, clarity, and love. This journey, with all its patience and purity, offers healing not just for the individual, but for the generations yet to come.

Chapter 13: Ayurveda and Women's Sexual Health

In the sacred literature of Ayurveda, the essence of life is understood through a deeply interconnected lens—where the body, mind, emotions, and spirit are not separate entities, but vibrating expressions of one continuous field of consciousness. Among the foundational pillars of human life are Dharma (righteous living), Artha (pursuit of livelihood), Kama (pursuit of desires and pleasures), and Moksha (liberation of the soul). Within this framework, Kama is not an indulgence but a sacred expression of longing, intimacy, creativity, and sensual fulfillment. It represents the inherent human drive to seek connection, to feel deeply, and to experience joy through union—whether emotional, physical, or spiritual. In the Ayurvedic vision, sexuality is an act of harmony, of reverence for the self and the other, and when approached with awareness, it becomes a powerful channel for healing and transformation. For women, whose emotional, hormonal, and creative rhythms are closely linked to nature, the honoring of sexuality is essential to well-being. It is not merely about reproductive capacity or desire—it is about vibrancy, presence, emotional openness, and embodiment of one's full feminine potential.

Ayurveda does not isolate sexual health from the rest of the body's systems—it views it as the refined expression of every other system functioning well. The reproductive tissue, known as Shukra in men and Artava in women, is considered the final and most precious refinement of the seven dhatus or bodily tissues. It is said that only when the prior six tissues—Rasa (plasma), Rakta (blood), Mamsa (muscle), Meda (fat), Asthi (bone), and Majja (marrow)—are fully nourished, does the Shukra dhatu form in abundance and quality. This indicates that sexual health is not just about hormones or reproductive organs; it reflects the overall state of nutrition, strength, digestion, emotional harmony, and mental clarity. When a woman feels depleted, disconnected, unsupported, or emotionally suppressed, her sexual vitality wanes—not as a failure, but as an intelligent reflection of deeper imbalances needing attention. Conversely, when a woman feels seen, safe, nourished, and emotionally integrated, her sensual energy flows effortlessly, even radiantly. This flow is not bound by age or reproductive capacity—it is a timeless inner rhythm of creative life force.

To understand a woman's sexual experience, Ayurveda asks us to look first at the doshas. Each dosha expresses desire, intimacy, and arousal in its own way. A Vata-dominant woman may experience fluctuations in desire, heightened sensitivity, and a tendency toward anxiety or fear in intimate contexts. Her touch must be gentle, her environment warm and emotionally secure, and her rhythm slow and grounding. She may benefit from daily oil massage with sesame oil, nourishing foods, regular routines, and consistent emotional support to stabilize her nervous system and enhance sensual receptivity. A Pitta-type woman, driven by intensity and passion, may exhibit a strong libido but also impatience, frustration, or a sharp tongue when emotionally unmet. She needs cooling, soothing, emotionally intelligent connection, and calming herbs like Shatavari, rose, or Yashtimadhu to balance her internal fire. A Kapha woman, naturally sensual and nurturing, may have stable desire but a tendency toward stagnation, emotional withdrawal, or low motivation. She thrives on stimulation, warmth, playful engagement, and invigorating spices and herbs like ginger, cinnamon, or Trikatu to energize her sensual circuits. These constitutional insights remind us that there is no one-size-fits-all approach to female sexuality; each woman must be seen and supported as a unique manifestation of nature's intelligence.

At the root of many sexual health challenges lies hormonal imbalance—an increasingly common issue due to stress, poor sleep, improper diet, overuse of stimulants or contraceptives, and emotional overload. Irregular cycles, painful menstruation, vaginal dryness, low libido, infertility, and even disinterest in intimacy are often linked to hormonal disruptions. Ayurveda approaches these issues not with suppressive medication but by restoring balance through rhythm, nourishment, and herbs that regulate the endocrine system holistically. Rejuvenating herbs like Shatavari nourish the reproductive tissues, increase moisture, balance estrogen, and calm the mind. Ashwagandha reduces cortisol, increases stamina, and supports thyroid and adrenal health—critical components in the hormonal web. Gokshura strengthens the urogenital tract, and Guduchi improves liver function, supporting detoxification and hormonal recycling. These herbs work slowly, respectfully, and deeply, aligning the body's inner intelligence with nature's rhythms.

Yet Ayurveda also understands that sexual vitality is not only physical or hormonal—it is profoundly emotional.

Many women, especially in modern urban lives, carry emotional wounds related to body image, consent, guilt, shame, or cultural conditioning. These impressions—known as Samskaras—can remain imprinted in the subtle tissues, particularly in the pelvic region. They may show up as chronic tension, numbness, pain during intercourse, an inability to relax or trust, or even aversion to intimacy. Rather than pathologize these experiences, Ayurveda offers deep compassion and therapies that honor the woman's journey back to herself. One such practice is Yoni Abhyanga, the gentle self-application of warm medicated oils to the pelvic area, which brings both physical nourishment and emotional integration. Another is Yoni Pichu, where a cotton swab soaked in cooling or toning herbal oil is placed within the vaginal canal to support healing, moisture, and comfort. Basti therapies—particularly Matra Basti with medicated oil—nourish the pelvic nerves, calm Vata, and restore balance. These sacred therapies are not merely mechanical—they are rituals of reconnection, encouraging women to feel, to listen, to reclaim parts of their bodies long ignored or shamed.

In matters of desire and intimacy, Ayurveda offers Vajikarana Rasayana—the science of aphrodisiac rejuvenation. But unlike modern stimulants, Ayurvedic aphrodisiacs aim to support the foundation: increasing Ojas (vital energy), enhancing Sattva (mental clarity), and opening Hridaya (the heart center). Herbs such as Bala, Safed Musli, Kapikacchu, and Vidari Kand are used to strengthen the tissues and increase pleasure. Rose, jasmine, cardamom, nutmeg, and saffron are used to awaken the senses, uplift the mood, and connect body and spirit. Oils like Brahmi taila, Bala taila, and Dhanvantaram taila are used for massage to circulate energy and relax the nerves. Diet also plays a major role. Sweet, unctuous, warming foods like dates, ghee, milk, soaked almonds, mung dal, and rice puddings infused with saffron or cardamom not only nourish Shukra and Artava but invite softness, sensuality, and inner glow. Fasting, cold foods, dry crackers, and erratic eating are discouraged, as they aggravate Vata and weaken hormonal fire.

Sexual disorders such as anorgasmia, lack of arousal, vaginismus, or low libido are approached not as isolated problems but as symptoms of deeper disharmony. A woman may experience these challenges due to unresolved trauma, lack of trust, hormonal insufficiency, depleted Ojas, or even suppressed creativity. The healing may involve Rasayana therapy, restorative yoga, pranayama, meditation, counseling, art therapy, or sacred rituals. Nothing is forced; everything is invited. Ayurveda encourages the woman to become her own healer, to listen without judgment, and to return to her natural state of joy and self-expression.

The psychological aspect of sexual health is further emphasized in Ayurveda through the concept of Kama Shastra—the science of sacred sensuality. It teaches that true intimacy is cultivated, not hurried. That a woman's arousal begins long before physical contact—with a look, a word, a moment of safety, a shared silence. That the bedroom is not merely a site of activity but a sanctuary of presence. That touch, breath, fragrance, and gaze are powerful tools of communion. And that when a woman feels honored, unrushed, and truly seen, her body becomes a gateway to transcendence.

The cultural silence around female desire has created generations of confusion, suppression, and shame. Ayurveda breaks this silence with wisdom, not rebellion. It does not ask women to become aggressive or dismissive of their past, but to come home to themselves gently. To recognize that sexual desire is not a flaw but a sacred fire. That when tended with love, awareness, and grace, it becomes a pathway to healing, wholeness, and divine union.

In the Ayurvedic tradition, women are seen as carriers of Shakti—the creative force of the universe. Their sexuality is not just a means of pleasure or reproduction; it is a portal to life itself. To reclaim this space is not an act of ego but an offering to the sacred. Through self-care, emotional honesty, proper nourishment, healing herbs, supportive relationships, and spiritual practice, a woman can awaken her sexual essence—not as a role to play, but as a truth to embody.

Ayurveda invites every woman to understand her sexual health not in isolation but as part of a beautiful continuum of her being. From menarche to menopause, from maiden to mother to mystic, each phase offers a new rhythm, a new awakening, a new invitation to embrace her body with reverence. Her pleasure is her power, her awareness is her medicine, and her embodied joy is her gift to the world. Through Ayurveda, she learns not only how to heal but how to flourish—fully, fearlessly, and in the luminous truth of her sensual sacred self.

Chapter 14: Ayurveda for Working and Urban Women

In today's fast-evolving world, the life of a working and urban woman is filled with movement, responsibility, and a kind of intensity that generations past may have never imagined. Balancing professional aspirations with domestic duties, nurturing relationships, managing finances, navigating technology, and trying to maintain self-care is a relentless cycle that often leaves women depleted—not only physically but emotionally, mentally, and spiritually. The rhythm of urban life is marked by noise, speed, and constant external demands. Amid all this, Ayurveda enters not as a cure-all pill or a strict doctrine, but as a quiet whisper of wisdom—guiding the woman back to her own nature, inviting her to listen to the voice of balance that still exists within, even when the world outside is spinning.

The ancient Ayurvedic seers may never have known what it feels like to sit through traffic while answering work emails on a mobile phone, or to pump breast milk during a lunch break, or to lead a boardroom discussion while silently managing menstrual cramps. Yet their teachings were created with the foresight to understand imbalance, overstimulation, and inner disconnect. They understood that the body is a reflection of the environment, and that when we move too fast, eat without presence, sleep irregularly, suppress emotions, or ignore inner rhythms, disease and distress naturally follow. Ayurveda teaches us that health is not merely the absence of illness, but the presence of vitality, clarity, joy, and harmony between our inner and outer worlds. For the working woman, who lives largely in the outer world of deadlines, calendars, social roles, and achievement, this is a crucial reminder.

Ayurveda begins with rhythm—daily rhythm, seasonal rhythm, life-stage rhythm. But in the cityscape, these rhythms are often replaced with artificial cycles of productivity, caffeine highs, late-night work sessions, social media scrolling, and a constant sense of being 'on. 'In this context, the absence of rhythm becomes one of the greatest sources of imbalance. A woman who wakes at different hours each day, skips meals, eats while working, travels frequently, sleeps late, and juggles three to four roles simultaneously is not just functioning against her hormonal and digestive needs—she is gradually draining her ojas, her essence, her capacity to sustain joy and resilience. The Vata dosha—the subtle energy of movement and change—becomes predominant in this lifestyle. When unbalanced, it leads to dryness, fatigue, anxiety, insomnia, poor digestion, and emotional fragility. The antidote lies not in withdrawal, but in conscious regulation. Ayurveda encourages even the busiest woman to reclaim small pockets of ritual—whether it's waking consistently at dawn, applying warm oil to the feet before bed, drinking cumin-coriander-fennel tea daily, or eating her meals sitting down without distractions.

When a woman begins her day with mindfulness—even a few minutes of silence, gratitude, or intentional breath—she establishes the tone for her nervous system. This momentary pause before entering the outer world allows her to check in with her body, set her intention, and protect her emotional boundaries. The day may still bring its chaos, but the way she meets it is different—more grounded, more centered, more whole. Urban life can strip away this centering force unless actively nurtured. The sensory overload of digital devices, screens, loud environments, and fast-paced speech fragments attention and disorients the mind. Ayurveda responds by recommending sensory nourishment: gazing at the rising sun, smelling soothing essential oils, eating with the hands, massaging the scalp, listening to soft music, or walking barefoot on grass. These acts, though simple, reconnect the woman to her sensory intelligence, which in turn regulates her endocrine and nervous systems.

Nutrition is another area where working women face tremendous challenges. Despite increasing awareness around healthy eating, many urban women struggle to maintain a consistent, nourishing food routine. They may start their day with coffee on an empty stomach, skip breakfast entirely, eat lunch at their desk in between tasks, binge on snacks late afternoon, and have a heavy dinner at 9 or 10 p.m. while catching up on work or entertainment. Such a pattern is a recipe for metabolic disruption, hormonal imbalance, and emotional instability. Ayurveda teaches that digestion is the key to all health. If Agni—the digestive fire—is weak, then even the most organic food becomes a source of toxins (ama). Women are advised to honor their hunger cues, eat freshly cooked meals at regular times, and choose foods appropriate to their dosha and the season. Warm, soft, and oily foods stabilize Vata. Cooling, light, and mildly spiced foods pacify Pitta. Light, dry, and stimulating foods reduce Kapha. Herbs like ginger, cumin, ajwain, and turmeric can be kept in small travel kits or sprinkled over meals to improve digestion. Even a spoonful of ghee in dal, a pinch of rock salt in lemon water, or a warm drink after lunch can transform the way the body absorbs and assimilates nourishment.

One of the most common health challenges faced by working women is stress. Not just the dramatic stress of crisis or conflict, but the chronic, low-grade stress of juggling too much for too long without pause. This constant mental overdrive affects the hypothalamic-pituitary-adrenal axis, leading to issues like irregular periods, PCOS, hair fall, fatigue, mood swings, and lowered immunity. Ayurveda views the mind and body as inseparable. Mental stress directly affects the doshas—especially Vata and Pitta—and leads to poor digestion, skin breakouts, lowered libido, insomnia, and emotional reactivity. To counter this, Ayurveda prescribes mental rest as seriously as it does physical rest. Resting does not mean laziness—it means withdrawing attention from external engagement and returning inward. Practices like meditation, yoga nidra, slow walks without devices, or even five minutes of deep belly breathing can begin to reset the system. At the workplace, taking short breaks to breathe consciously, stretch gently, or close the eyes for a few moments can act as nervous system resets. Carrying a calming herbal blend like brahmi, jatamansi, or tulsi in tea form or capsule can help manage workplace reactivity and boost mental endurance.

Another dimension where Ayurveda supports the urban woman is in emotional health. The pressures to conform, to be constantly productive, attractive, available, or competitive can fracture a woman's emotional landscape. She may suppress her emotions to appear strong, bottle up grief to be seen as efficient, or disconnect from her body to meet societal expectations. Ayurveda urges her to return to emotional honesty. Emotions are not enemies—they are messengers. Suppressed anger may turn into inflammation. Buried grief may manifest as depression. Chronic worry may lead to digestive disorders. Ayurveda offers therapies like Shirodhara, nasya, abhyanga, and marma to release these emotional blocks gently. It also encourages journaling, chanting, silence, sacred art, and talking to trusted friends or counselors. A woman who can feel her emotions without drowning in them becomes deeply empowered—not because she controls everything, but because she understands her inner weather and adjusts accordingly.

For women who travel frequently, Ayurveda offers specific guidance to counterbalance Vata aggravation. Travel—especially air travel—causes dryness, constipation, fatigue, and insomnia. Drinking warm water or ginger tea during the journey, applying oil to the ears and nostrils before flights, wearing natural fabrics, and practicing gentle stretches upon arrival can help mitigate these effects. Eating warm, moist, and familiar foods post-travel stabilizes digestion. A grounding bath or self-massage resets the body. When travel becomes routine, carrying herbs like triphala, ashwagandha, or hingvastak churna becomes a vital act of self-care, ensuring the woman remains anchored no matter where she goes.

One of the deepest offerings of Ayurveda to working women is the concept of inner alignment over outer performance. Modern life teaches women to measure their worth through productivity, appearances, or approval.

Ayurveda shifts this narrative. It tells her that when she is aligned—when her sleep is sound, her digestion strong, her breath calm, her cycle regular, her emotions honored, and her heart open—she will naturally perform with grace, lead with clarity, and love with resilience. She doesn't need to push constantly; she needs to flow, to trust, and to rest. She doesn't need to fix everything in a day; she needs to begin with one small change, one loving habit, one moment of stillness. Ayurveda does not ask her to give up her career, ambition, or dreams. It simply asks her to not lose herself in their pursuit.

The urban woman is powerful not because she does everything, but because she knows when to pause, when to delegate, when to say no, and when to choose peace over pressure. She is radiant not because of cosmetics or clothing, but because of her inner fire—her Agni—burning bright and steady. She is graceful not because she follows trends, but because she lives in tune with her own truth. Ayurveda is her ally, her friend, her mirror. It is not a rigid system, but a compassionate path—a set of tools, rituals, herbs, and insights that gently bring her back to herself. It tells her that her body is wise, her emotions valid, her rhythms sacred, and her health non-negotiable.

In the middle of traffic, she can place a drop of rose oil on her wrist. Between meetings, she can sip warm herbal water with reverence. After a long day, she can oil her feet and rest in silence. These are not indulgences. They are survival, strength, and sacred rebellion. In a world that rewards hustle, the woman who slows down to nourish herself is revolutionary. She reclaims her well-being not just for herself, but for everyone she touches—her family, her colleagues, her community, and her future self. Ayurveda empowers her to do this—not through demands, but through remembrance. It reminds her: you are not here to survive the city. You are here to thrive, to shine, to rest, and to rise again—in balance, in rhythm, and in radiant wellness.

Chapter 15: Ayurveda for the Modern Woman: Integration and Transformation

In the noise of modern living, with its relentless demands and unyielding pace, many women find themselves striving harder while feeling more disconnected from their own bodies, emotions, and inner rhythm. Amid the pressure to succeed, care for others, stay connected online, look a certain way, and push through fatigue and discomfort, there often remains little space for the deeper inquiry into how one truly feels. What starts as ambition can, over time, lead to exhaustion. What begins as multitasking can turn into fragmentation. In such a climate, wellness is no longer a luxury—it becomes a survival necessity. Yet, the mainstream narrative around health often centers on superficial fixes, quick results, and chasing external ideals. It is here that Ayurveda offers a different paradigm, a quieter but more enduring path that leads not just to relief from symptoms, but to transformation—one that begins within and honors every layer of a woman's being.

Ayurveda, in its essence, is the art of remembering. Remembering how the body feels when it is rested and not rushed. Remembering how food tastes when eaten with attention. Remembering how breath becomes a balm when one allows it to deepen. Remembering how each woman is a reflection of nature herself—cyclical, adaptive, intuitive, powerful, and worthy of nourishment, rest, and rhythm. For the modern woman, integration does not mean returning to a lifestyle that mimics the past. Rather, it means carrying the wisdom of Ayurveda into the very heart of contemporary life—into the cubicles and boardrooms, into smartphones and traffic jams, into parenting and partnerships, into kitchen shelves and travel bags. The tools of Ayurveda are timeless because they meet the human being, not the setting. Whether in a Himalayan village or a New York City apartment, the laws of digestion, breath, emotional flow, sleep, and stress remain unchanged. What differs is how consciously we choose to work with them.

The journey of transformation begins with the simple but profound act of self-awareness. It is the willingness to observe—not critically, but compassionately. A woman who becomes curious about her own body begins to understand the language of symptoms not as disruptions, but as conversations. A headache after skipped meals, bloating after a cold drink, heaviness after emotional avoidance—these are the body's way of requesting attention. Ayurveda calls this prajnaparadha—the failure of the intellect to heed the body's signals. In restoring this inner listening, Ayurveda asks no woman to be perfect, only to be present. Presence begins with asking gentle questions: Am I hungry or just bored? Am I angry or afraid? Am I tired or overwhelmed? What would nourish me right now? Over time, this simple practice of turning inward cultivates a level of attunement that no lab test can replace. Self-awareness, then, becomes the first and most powerful medicine.

For the modern woman already engaged in conventional healthcare—perhaps taking medication for thyroid, undergoing fertility treatment, managing autoimmune disorders, or recovering from surgery—Ayurveda does not oppose but supports. It expands the lens. It brings in the context of lifestyle, diet, stress, relationships, and emotional patterns that often go unaddressed in allopathic treatment. A woman with hormonal imbalances may take pills, but if her meals are erratic, her sleep poor, and her self-worth tied to productivity, the imbalance may persist or return. Ayurveda steps in not to reject modern tools but to complete the circle. It works upstream—balancing doshas, cleansing ama (toxins), restoring agni (digestive fire), and rejuvenating dhatus (tissues). It asks not only what the disease is, but why it arose, and how the system can be strengthened from its root.

This integration does not demand that the woman choose between East and West. Rather, it invites her to become the center of her own healing story. To walk into a doctor's office with informed questions. To seek counseling when emotions overwhelm. To use herbs and foods as daily support rather than reactive correction. To consider both test results and intuition, both science and spirit. This integrative lens allows a woman to feel empowered—not just compliant. She is no longer a passive patient; she becomes an active participant, a sovereign steward of her body, her choices, and her healing journey.

But transformation is not sustained by information alone. It requires consistency, patience, and tools that can be returned to, day after day. Ayurveda excels in providing these tools—not in overwhelming complexity, but in simplicity that adapts to life. A cup of warm water upon waking. A few minutes of abhyanga before the shower. Eating meals at regular times. Taking a mindful pause before reacting. Going to bed before 10 p.m. Each of these actions may seem insignificant, but their cumulative effect is profound. The body, when offered rhythm, begins to repair itself. The mind, when offered pause, begins to unclutter. The emotions, when acknowledged, begin to move. The nervous system, when respected, begins to regulate. And from this slow and steady ground, a woman begins to experience energy not from stimulation, but from alignment.

The seasonal dimension of Ayurveda further enriches this long-term wellness. By attuning to the qualities of the external environment—heat, cold, dryness, dampness—a woman can make micro-adjustments that prevent disease before it begins. In summer, she favors cooling foods, lighter oils, and early meals. In winter, she adds warmth, spice, and grounding rituals. During seasonal transitions, she detoxes gently, cleanses the channels, and rests more. These adjustments are not rules—they are intelligent responses to nature. The modern woman need not overhaul her life; she need only observe and respond. When she understands her own dosha, and how it interacts with seasonal and emotional factors, she gains a level of mastery over her well-being that is both intuitive and scientific.

But even with all the right routines, herbs, and awareness, true transformation arises when a woman reclaims her story. Too often, women are taught to override their instincts, to ignore pain, to keep moving despite fatigue, to minimize their needs, to apologize for their desires. Ayurveda dismantles this narrative. It says: Your needs are sacred. Your body is not a burden. Your emotions are valid. Your rest is productive. Your pleasure is healing. Your softness is strength. And your intuition is wise. In reclaiming this story, a woman heals not just herself but the collective. She teaches her daughters that cycles are beautiful. She teaches her peers that boundaries are self-love. She teaches her partners that communication is connection. She teaches herself that silence is not absence—it is medicine.

This transformation does not require a perfect life. It thrives in real life—with all its mess, complexity, and imperfection. It invites the modern woman to bring Ayurveda into her everyday reality, whether she is managing a household, leading a company, studying late, raising children, or caring for aging parents. It gives her the permission to be slow in a fast world. To say no when depleted. To cry when needed. To laugh without guilt. To nap when tired. To cook as a ritual. To walk without headphones. To greet her body not with criticism, but with gratitude. And in doing so, she does not withdraw from the world—she engages it more powerfully, more consciously, more compassionately.

As this book reaches its close, the message of Ayurveda to every woman is simple: Begin where you are. You do not need to do it all at once. You do not need to get it perfect. You do not need exotic ingredients or complex protocols. You need presence. You need rhythm. You need honesty. Begin with one habit. Begin with one breath. Begin with noticing the way your body responds to what you feed it, how your energy changes with who you spend time with, how your emotions rise and fall with your monthly cycle. Let each observation become a seed of self-awareness. Let each act of care become a thread in the tapestry of your well-being.

In a world that often asks women to give everything, Ayurveda gives her back to herself. And in that return, she does not lose her ambition—she redefines it. Success becomes about sustainability. Beauty becomes about radiance. Strength becomes about softness. Productivity becomes about presence. And health becomes about wholeness.

This is the transformation that Ayurveda offers—not a prescription, but a remembering. A way of living that honors the complexity of modern life while anchoring in the wisdom of nature. A way of being that is fierce and gentle, structured and intuitive, grounded and free. A way of healing that does not rush but roots. A way of wellness that does not isolate but integrates.

In the end, the modern woman is not separate from the ancient woman. She is her daughter. Her continuation. Her evolution. The same cycles live in her womb. The same earth feeds her cells. The same moon pulls her tides. The same breath carries her prayers. When she embraces this lineage—when she lives Ayurveda not as a theory but as a living practice—she becomes medicine, not just for herself, but for her family, her community, her world.

And in that, she finds not only integration. She finds home.

Appendices

From the Book: Ayurveda for Women's Wellness

The appendices serve as a practical guide and reference extension to the main content of the book, offering readers applied tools and terminology that complement Ayurvedic understanding in daily life. This section is designed to deepen the reader's engagement with Ayurvedic wisdom, especially as it applies to women's wellness.

The glossary of Ayurvedic terms includes essential concepts and Sanskrit words commonly used throughout the book. Words such as Dosha, Agni, Ama, Dhatu, Srotas, Ojas, and Prakruti are foundational to Ayurvedic science. For example, "Dosha" refers to the three biological energies—Vata, Pitta, and Kapha—that govern the body's constitution and functions. "Agni" is the digestive fire, critical to metabolism and immunity. "Ama" represents undigested toxins that accumulate in the body and cause disease. A clear understanding of these terms is vital for integrating Ayurvedic principles into lifestyle and healthcare decisions.

The daily routine chart, or Dinacharya, provides a structured outline for women to align their daily activities with natural rhythms. This chart includes ideal times for waking up, cleansing, meditation, exercise, meals, work, and sleep. Following such a routine helps balance hormonal functions, improves digestion, enhances emotional stability, and cultivates inner awareness. For example, rising before sunrise and practicing gentle yoga or walking can enhance Vata balance and mental clarity, especially for women dealing with irregular menstrual cycles or anxiety. Regular mealtimes and early dinners support Pitta and Kapha, reducing bloating and lethargy.

A recommended herbs list has been included for everyday women's health concerns. These herbs are categorized by their supportive actions—such as adaptogens, hormone regulators, digestive aids, and calming agents. Notable examples include Shatavari (for reproductive and hormonal support), Ashwagandha (for stress and vitality), Triphala (for digestion and detox), Brahmi (for mental clarity), and Lodhra (for uterine health). Each herb's Sanskrit name, Latin botanical name, primary action, and usage method is concisely described. This resource is designed to empower women to incorporate gentle, natural healing aids into their routine under proper guidance.

Ayurvedic assessment tools, particularly Prakriti analysis, allow individuals to determine their constitutional type. Knowing one's Prakriti—Vata, Pitta, Kapha, or a combination—enables personalized dietary, lifestyle, and therapeutic recommendations. The appendix offers a simplified questionnaire to help readers identify their doshic balance. It covers questions related to body frame, skin type, emotional tendencies, digestion, energy levels, and sleep patterns. While this tool does not replace professional Ayurvedic consultation, it provides a useful starting point for self-awareness and informed decision-making. Understanding Prakriti is key to addressing women's unique transitions—menstruation, pregnancy, menopause—with mindfulness and balance.

Together, these appendices transform the theoretical insights of Ayurveda into accessible, daily practices. They act as a bridge between timeless wisdom and modern women's wellness needs, supporting a life of harmony, vitality, and conscious living.